# DANCING
## on a
# VOLCANO

# DANCING
## on a
# VOLCANO

### The Latin American Drug Trade

### Scott B. MacDonald

PRAEGER

New York
Westport, Connecticut
London

**Library of Congress Cataloging-in-Publication Data**

MacDonald, Scott.
    Dancing on a volcano : the Latin American drug trade / Scott B.
MacDonald.
      p.     cm.
    Bibliography: p.
    Includes index.
    ISBN 0-275-92752-0 (alk. paper)
    ISBN 0-275-93105-6 (pbk : alk. paper)
    1. Drug traffic—Latin America.   2. Drug traffic—United States.
I. Title.
HV5840.L3M34    1988
363.4'5'098—dc19        88-9950

Library of Congress Catalog Card Number: 88-9950
ISBN: 0-275-92752-0
ISBN: 0-275-93105-6 (paperback)

First published in 1988

Praeger Publishers, One Madison Avenue, New York, NY 10010
An imprint of Greenwood Publishing Group, Inc.

Printed in the United States of America

The paper used in this book complies with the Permanent
Paper Standard issued by the National Information Standards
Organization (Z39.48—1984).

10  9  8  7  6  5  4  3  2

To

my wife,
Kateri Scott-MacDonald,

my mother,
Anita B. MacDonald,

and

my editor,
Susan Pazourek

# Contents

# Preface

Research for this book began three years ago in 1985. At the time, I was the Unit Manager of the International and Specialized Industry Group and Senior Country Risk Analyst at Connecticut National Bank. Part of my responsibilities entailed the study of major economic and financial trends in a number of Latin American countries. By 1985, it had become apparent that the amount of capital involved in the Latin American drug trade was enormous. I became curious about the impact of the drug trade, especially with regard to the debt crisis. In an initial study, accomplished with the assistance of Edward J. Tregurtha, I sought to answer (or at least explore the parameters of) a number of questions. What was the impact of the drug trade on Latin America and the Caribbean? How was the trade structured, or put another way—who got what and why? Did different countries play different roles? How far had the drug trade permeated Latin American society? This study demonstrated three things: (1) Only the surface of the problem had been scratched; (2) there was not an extensive literature on the political and economic aspects of the drug trade in the 1980s; and (3) the drug trade, as an $80–$150 billion business, clearly had a major political and socioeconomic impact.

Three years later, I still admit to not having enough information. Though awareness of the illicit drug trade has grown, the literature remains underdeveloped. There are a number of reasons for this: (1) drugs are a highly sensitive and potentially sensational topic, capable of gaining media headlines and causing tensions between governments; (2) the collection of first-hand data can be hazardous; and (3) because of the nature of the drug trade, good reliable statistical data is difficult to acquire. An additional point is that the data that does exist is often suspect. These conditions have therefore left the field open mainly to the more intrepid journalists. There are some excellent studies, such as Melanie Creagan Dreher's *Working Men and Ganja* (1982) and *Cocoa and Cocaine: Effects on People and Policy in Latin America* (1986), edited by Deborah Pacini and Christine Franquemont; but in general scholarly research has lagged behind the pace of events. This book seeks to bridge at least part of this information gap, offering the reader a comprehensive picture of the Latin American drug trade.

In the three years that have gone into the research and writing of this book, I have benefited from the insights and encouragement of a number of people in the United States, the Caribbean, Colombia, Brazil, Mexico, and Venezuela. In expressing my gratitude, I begin with my uncle, Dr. Loftus Walton, a doctor who has worked with drug patients in Connecticut. He was an initial source of inspiration in pushing forward with the project. I owe a great deal of gratitude to Clarence Moore, editor and owner of the *Times of the Americas.* He has provided insights into Latin America, has always been ready to discuss ideas, and, most of all, gave me a place to work at a time when I was between jobs. Dr. Georges Fauriol at the Center for Strategic and International Studies has also been a friend and colleague who has suggested ideas and provided encouragement to forge ahead. Along the same lines, I must express thanks to Dr. Timothy Ashby, Director of the Mexican and Caribbean Basin Desk, at the International Trade Agency, and Bruce Zagaris, a Washington-based lawyer with a shared love for the Caribbean. Both men suffered through various drafts and discussions on the topic.

A number of other individuals require special notation. I thank Barbara Bennett and Larry Simoneaux, fellow bankers, and Nancy Tracewell, journalist, for reading and editing the entire manuscript; Eva Loser, at the Center for Strategic and International Studies, for her comments on the chapter dealing with Panama; and my mother, Anita B. MacDonald, for being a loyal fan and reader. I have also benefitted from discussions on Latin America and the drug trade with Francis "Bud" Mullen, former head of the Drug Enforcement Agency (DEA), Bill Perry, Albert L. Gastmann, Uwe Bott, and Norman Bailey. Extra-special thanks go to two women: my wife, Kateri, who has always been an inspiration and a tough critic, and my intern, Laura Vásquez, who helped in the research and typing of certain chapters.

This book was written with malice to none. I am aware of the sensitivity of the drug issue throughout the region and strongly feel it is a universal problem, that everyone in the Americas must confront. The author takes sole responsibility for errors in this book. The author has also sought to provide as up-to-date as possible an account of the Latin American drug trade. At the same time, the danger exists of being overtaken by events, which is amply demonstrated by events in Panama in 1988. I hope that in providing a comprehensive study of this subject a positive step has been taken in enhancing awareness of a problem shared by almost all societies of the Americas.

# DANCING
## on a
# VOLCANO

# 1

# Dancing on a Volcano: The Latin American Drug Trade

## INTRODUCTION

In the late 1980s, the Latin American drug trade encompasses most of the Western Hemisphere, ranging from the major coca producers in Bolivia and Peru, to Colombia, the volcano's core, through Venezuela and the Caribbean transit countries, and finally, to the world's largest and most lucrative market, the United States. To a lesser extent, Canada is also an important destination. Despite efforts to curb the spread of the Latin American drug trade, marijuana, heroin, and cocaine continue to enter the United States. Cocaine, in particular, has become a major problem and its production has expanded from its traditional "homelands" of Bolivia, Colombia and Peru, to Venezuela, Ecuador, and western Brazil. Altogether, the Latin American drug trade has complicated relations between the United States and many of its southern neighbors over a plethora of issues, ranging from offshore banking privacy rights related to the laundering of "dirty money," narcotics enforcement, corruption, the search for alternative crops, and international terrorism.

The purpose of this book is to examine the Latin American drug trade; it probably will continue to be a major problem through the rest of the decade for the United States as well as for a growing number of Latin American nations. The focus is limited to cocaine, marijuana, and heroin and places an emphasis on the early 1980s to mid–1988. The United States and its southern neighbors face growing addict populations, high crime rates, and a costly drain of government revenues to combat the trade's negative effects; revenues which should be used for other important social programs, such as education and health care. Added to these concerns are the interrelated issues of Latin American indebtedness, the rise of protectionism in international trade, and the East-West struggle. It is difficult for many nations, hard-pressed by debt repayment obligations to divert their scarce funds to combat powerful drug merchants who are sometimes militarily better equipped than government forces, who provide employment for thousands, and who bring in, albeit illegally, badly needed foreign exchange.

The rise of protectionism may exclude important Latin American exports from United States markets, hence reducing legal revenues and creating animosity vis-à-vis Washington in a crucially strategic region. Moreover, as Latin American states have economic difficulties, the survival of democratic governments could well be undermined by a combination of excessive debt obligations, United States trade protectionism, and the rise of powerful drug barons who have few qualms about forming "drug-insurgency nexuses" with leftist guerrillas like M–19 in Colombia. As Cuba has been an active middleman in the drug trade, the specter of the East-West struggle looms in the background. The stakes are high as the prize is the next several generations of youth in the Western Hemisphere and, indirectly, the balance of power in the Americas. In a sense, North and South Americans are together dancing on a volcano that may erupt, causing destruction on both individual and systemic levels.

The approach of this study is historical; the second chapter examines the background of drugs in Latin America. Colombia and Mexico, due to their importance as producers and exporters, each receive separate chapters, followed by chapters on Bolivia and Peru, the Caribbean marijuana producers (Belize and Jamaica), and the transit states (i.e., the Bahamas and Panama). Further chapters analyze the Cuban role; the impact on United States policy in the region; the interrelationship with the debt crisis; and possible solutions to the problem. This approach is justified by the lack of ready information on these topics for the general reader and by the narrowing of the geographical focus to the Americas. Two of the major studies, Brian Freemantle's *The Fix: Inside the World Drug Trade* and James Mills' *The Underground Empire: Where Crime and Governments Embrace* seek to be all-encompassing, including coverage of Asia's "Golden Triangle" and aspects of the trade in Africa and Europe as well as in the Americas.[1] Of the two studies, Freemantle's was more scholarly, easier to read, and accessible to the general reader. Mills, in contrast, created a ponderous and, at times, difficult book to read, complete with an almost byzantine cast of characters. While Freemantle provides a valuable description of the global industry, Mills advances a thesis that emphasizes the hazy linkages between governments and the drug traders. Both provide food for thought, though *The Underground Empire* is an exercise in reading stamina. For the reader interested in the Latin American drug trade, both books provide a very general overview, colored with certain individual cases. While this approach does have value, it leaves the picture incomplete and a detailed analysis of the Latin American trade is wanting.

A growing mountain of official studies exist, but the information available is not in a readily digestible form and has been written with a relatively small audience in mind. Although a considerable amount of this study has been conducted through the lens of a social scientist, the audience is clearly intended to be much wider, seeking to answer some of the questions about what is rapidly becoming one of the major issues in inter-American relations. As the Latin American drug trade will continue to be an important factor through the 1980s and into the 1990s, it is crucial to have a better comprehension of its parameters and some of its complexities.

## THE SCOPE OF THE PROBLEM

Illegal drugs, especially cocaine, are pouring into the United States at an unprecedented rate and one of the most evident results is a growing user population. All the cocaine, a third of the heroin, and close to 80 percent of the marijuana on the United States market comes from Latin America. Marijuana users number close to 20 million, regular cocaine users number 8–22 million, and heroin addicts, 500,000.[2]

Cocaine has become a major concern in the United States, reaching near epidemic proportions. The volume of the alkaloid entering the American market has expanded to somewhere between 54 and 71 tons in 1983, a figure which has more than doubled since the seventies. According to the Drug Enforcement Agency's annual *Narcotics Intelligence Estimate*, marijuana use declined by 3 percent and heroin by 1 percent in 1984, while cocaine use in the United States rose by 11 percent. As Rudolf W. Giuliani, the United States Attorney for the Southern District of New York noted: "I agree that cocaine has become a gigantic problem; there may be five, even ten times as many users today as there were a decade ago. And there is so much cocaine pouring into the country that the price has actually gone down."[3] Furthermore, the number of people with cocaine-related problems seeking admission to federally funded drug clinics climbed by 600 percent from 1976 to 1981, the date of the latest available figures.[4] The practice of free-basing (the inhaling of cocaine vapors instead of snorting or injecting this powerful stimulant of the central nervous system), has compounded the cocaine problem. It is a highly addictive and exceedingly debilitating practice.

In 1984 and 1985, all phases of trafficking—cultivation, processing and distribution—expanded and continued into 1986 and 1987. The following table, supplied by the State Department, partially reflects this.

**Coca Leaf Production (in metric tons)**

|  | 1986 | 1987 |
|---|---|---|
| Bolivia | 44,000–52,920 | 46,000–67,000 |
| Colombia | 12,000–13,600 | 18,000–23,000 |
| Peru | 95,000–120,000 | 98,000–121,000 |
| Ecuador | 1,000 | up to 400 |

In Latin America and the Caribbean, cocaine use has also reached critical levels alarming both government and health officials. According to the *1985 State Department International Narcotics Control Strategy Report*, 40,000–50,000 Bolivians, 150,000 Peruvians, and more than 600,000 Colombians have "serious" addiction problems. In Venezuela, government authorities have estimated that at least 150,000 people are regular users of drugs ranging from cocaine and *basuco* (a semi-processed cocaine paste used for smoking) to marijuana and methaqualone.[5] According to the National Health Ministry of Colombia, the estimated number of *basuco* smokers in early 1987 was more than 400,000. Mexico, Jamaica, and the Bahamas also have registered growing numbers of drug users.

Another dimension of the problem is that an increasing number of Latin American farmers have discovered that coca cultivation is far more lucrative than corn or other staple crops. Consequently, in the 1980s, the production of cocaine, heroin, and marijuna for export are gradually taking over fields formerly used for food crops. While this trend has been most severe in Bolivia and Peru, it has affected Colombia and parts of Jamaica, Belize, Ecuador, and Panama. Larry Deaton, an economist for the United States Department of Agriculture noted a major negative offshoot of this trend: "The irony is that while this diversion of land makes more money, it takes away basic crops in countries that already have food deficits."[6] Moreover, while drug exports earn badly needed foreign exchange, they also cause capital outflow as food must be imported to meet domestic needs.

The drug trade is also big business. It extends from the key cocaine producer states of Bolivia and Peru to Colombia which has often been described as the "linchpin." Colombia's fertile soil has produced vast amounts of marijuana and cocaine while it has functioned as an important transit point to northern markets.

Cocaine production has been reported in Ecuador, western Brazil, and Mexico. Mexico has also been a producer of marijuana and heroin; in the late 1980s this has become a tense issue between this nation and the United States. In the Caribbean, Jamaica and Belize have emerged as important marijuana growers, while the Bahamas, the Netherlands Antilles, and Venezuela have become key transit states. It is likely that the two island-states, along with the Cayman Islands and Turks and Caicos have also been used as offshore banking centers to launder drug money. Venezuela, long on the periphery of the drug network became a major bridge for shipments of Colombian cocaine bound for the United States in 1983, due to the tightening of United States controls over Colombian aircraft and vessels entering South Florida. Consequently, Colombian smugglers rerouted their cocaine cargoes through neighboring Venezuela. In most cases, the Venezuelan cocaine connection commences in Bolivia, where the coca is cultivated, is then flown to Manaus, Brazil, and then to Colombia where it is converted into cocaine in clandestine laboratories. There are similar facilities in western Brazil and Ecuador. Following that, it is sent across the border into Venezuela and north to the United States. Panama has also been added to the list of nations involved, both as a minor producer and transit point. Furthermore, both Cuba and Nicaragua are implicated in the drug trade, functioning as safe havens for dealers and supplying weapons to leftist guerrilla groups, such as M–19 in Colombia who protect the drug traders.

The current estimated value of the Latin American drug trade ranges from \$80–\$150 billion, most of which remains in the United States or is deposited in Swiss banks.[7] In many cases—Bolivia, Colombia, and Peru—drug exports earn more money that is returned to the country than do legal exports like coffee, tin, oil, and sugar. Those involved in the trade, referred to as *narcotraficantes* or cocaine cowboys, or drug barons, have created their own states within states providing the foundation for export-based economies, generating employment and carrying out a number of charitable deeds much in the tradition of a modern-day Robin Hood. As Rensselaer W. Lee, Jr. noted of what he calls the "drug-insurgency nexus":

> . . . drug barons today are major political forces in countries such as Bolivia, Colombia, and Peru, carving out states within states in coca-producing regions, sometimes forming alliances of convenience with local leftist guerrillas, undermining authorities with bribery and assassinations, and amassing enough armed might to keep governments at bay. Drug traffickers have also sought to play by the local political rules, banding together to lobby politicians to nominate candidates for public office and occasionally to negotiate with national leaders as quasi-equals.[8]

The drug-insurgency nexus, therefore, plays an important role in the Latin American drug trade. For the purposes of this study, the drug-insurgency nexus is the formation of political-military enclaves controlled by traffickers in alliance with leftist, revolutionary groups. "Narcoterrorism" is part of the equation. This means that the funding and equipping of terrorist (or revolutionary) activities—i.e., assassinations and hostage-taking, are accomplished by involvement in drug-related activities that may include the production, export and/or the production of narcotics. The drug-insurgency nexus is usually a "marriage of convenience" between drug traffickers and leftist insurgent groups. This does not mean that the *narcotraficantes* and leftist insurgents share an ideological perspective. To the contrary, the drug smugglers are usually conservative and status quo-oriented and the leftist groups are usually seeking to radically transform their respective societies by overthrowing their governments and implementing a revolutionary new order usually based on an offshoot of Marxist-Leninist ideology. It should also be added that the drug-insurgency nexus is not limited to Latin America, but is also in evidence elsewhere around the globe as in Lebanon's Bekka Valley.

In 1980–81, General García Meza, then leader of the ruling military junta in Bolivia, sought to use the military, the customs service, and local narcotics agencies to establish a monopoly over the coca trade in the major producing region of Chapare. The effort failed due to the resistance of militarily well-equipped coca growers and the political clout of their leaders. As one observer noted: "Customers and narcotics checkpoints on the highway which links the district with Cochabamba were dynamited, and patrols of paramilitaries were repeatedly ambushed by local farmers armed with modern rifles, machine-guns and even bazookas."[9]

This situation has changed only moderately since the 1980–81 period as reflected by an incident in January 1985 in which a camp of 245 antidrug police, known as the Leopards, were surrounded by about 17,000 coca farmers in the Chapare region. Due, in part, to United States pressure (threats to terminate all aid), the Leopards had made arrests and disrupted processing plants. The incident was ultimately resolved when the government threatened military intervention. Although the incident allegedly began over a rape, the response on the part of the peasants indicated the central government's inability to control the region or to avoid a confrontation with the powerful peasant groups linked to coca cultivation. Moreover, the involvement of American troops in antidrug operations in Bolivia in 1986 only temporarily stemmed the flow of drugs and no major drug figures were captured.

Another complicating factor in the Bolivian case is that the government of President Victor Paz Estenssoro complained of Cuban interference in his nation's internal affairs. Cuban officials had sought to develop better ties to peasant union leaders. The situation in Bolivia which has many of the elements of the drug-insurgency nexus and where government control is virtually nonexistent in key producing areas, is not alien to some regions of Belize, Brazil, Colombia, Ecuador, Jamaica, Peru, and Venezuela.

The wide scope of the Latin American drug trade is perhaps best exemplified by Peru. Alan García, who became president in 1985, inherited a nation characterized by severe economic contraction, inflation over 200 percent, an external debt of $14 billion, a leftist guerrilla insurgency (that of the Sendero Luminoso), and a strongly entrenched drug trade operating in the Peruvian Amazon.

In the 1970s, the export of coca and cocaine, estimated at $500 million annually, had become one of Peru's largest exports. The major market has been the United States, and previous governments had either turned a blind eye to the drug trade or were actively involved. The complexity of the drug trade in Peru, however, has made it exceedingly difficult to uproot (as in many regions of the mountainous interior), coca cultivation is the sole source of revenue. The large Indian population, which has been traditionally ignored by the succession of governments in Lima, has been heavily involved in the illegal trade. Consequently, that sector of Peruvian society has been most sensitive to antidrug trade campaigns. As Riordan Roett noted:

> When enforcement, eradication and crop substitution programs financed by the United States began in 1982, the local economy suffered. Soon, the Sendero guerrillas moved into the area to exploit native discontent. The antidrug program came to a halt when the armed forces moved into the region and said that they would fight subversion—the Sendero—but not narcotics. The cultivation resumed and grew.[10]

The drug-insurgency nexus remains a major problem in Peru, as the trade still continues despite government efforts. The Peruvian situation has been further complicated by other factors. While imposing austerity measures, the new president announced that he would limit debt repayments to only 10 percent of net export earnings, an action that did not sit well with the Latin American nation's international creditors. Allegedly during the same period of time that Peru's new government irritated both the United States government and the banking community, a drug baron, "Crazy Mosquito" offered to pay personally his nation's entire public debt; a tempting offer considering that the debt is a crushing burden on the country. Rumors abounded that some elements of the new administration were considering the legalization of cocaine for export only, if too much pressure was brought to bear on Peru to repay its loans. García, however has been most active in tackling the drug trade, purging the government, the police, and the military of tainted individuals, conducting joint antidrug maneuvers with Colombian forces in the area that has become known as the "Amazonian Triangle," and taking an active public stance on the issue. García's antiimperialist rhetoric, his active diplomacy in the Third World, and intransigence with his nation's creditors, have irritated the American government, yet his "get tough" stance on the drug trade has been appreciated. Moreover, Peru's strategic location in Latin America has not been lost on Washington. The complex intermixture of debt, drugs, and a leftist insurgency clearly underscores the wide scope of the Latin American drug trade.

## POINTING THE FINGER

Despite the commonality of increasing drug addiction and drug-related violence, North America blames South America for the problem and vice versa. There is, in fact, enough blame to go around for everyone. Furthermore, the problem is not going to disappear; rather it is going to intensify due to the rise of cocaine use in the United States, Canada, and Latin America. Whose problem is it: the United States which is the main market with a high demand or Latin America which is the major supplier, with its own growng user population?

In the early 1970s, when world demand for cocaine and other drugs expanded considerably, Latin American nations and certain transit states, such as the Bahamas, ignored the issue. Many felt it was a North American problem: demand in the United States stimulated production. The consensus was that the North Americans, with their millions of abusers and addicts, had no moral right to pin the blame for the drug trade on Latin Americans. As the former Colombian President Alfonso López (1974–78) commented: "It is the Americans who are corrupting us!" It was also cynically suggested in Colombia that marijuana should have been legalized: if there was no way of stopping the smuggling and the market continued to exist in North America, why bother trying to change the situation? In addition, the drug trade brought added revenues and employment to a number of otherwise economically depressed areas such as eastern Bolivia. It has been estimated that some $200–$300 million return to the Bolivian economy annually in the form of drug revenues. Despite official United States disapproval over Latin America's half-hearted efforts to stem the flow, the trade expanded. In the late 1970s and early 1980s, the nature of the problem changed as addiction rose in the producer countries. What had initially been perceived as a "gringo" problem had become a Latin problem.

From the North American perspective, the Latin American drug trade was caused by Latin Americans; it was their countries that were involved in the production of marijuana, cocaine, and heroin. Consequently, it was the Latin American nations that should be responsible for purging this destructive evil. The more the North Americans pushed for results, the more Latins became irritated by what they regarded as a policy of paternalism, and, in some radical circles, United States intervention. By the mid–1980s, United States irritation over the seeming indifference of some governments to the problem helped create a group in the United States Congress favoring diplomatic sanctions. In 1983, Congress passed an amendment requiring the president to suspend economic aid to countries that failed to take adequate measures to control the narcotics trade. As then Senator Paula Hawkins (R-Florida) commented in 1984: "Why should we give those countries any foreign aid if they are the source of all this poison? We're going to cut off their aid and shut them down."[11]

It is doubtful that diplomatic sanctions against selected Latin American nations would have any impact, except the negative outcome of perhaps helping cause a weak democratic government, as in Peru or Bolivia, to fall. Not only would this be counterproductive to combating the drug trade, it would also open the door to radical leftist forces that look toward Cuba and the Soviet Union as allies. Confrontation, in most respects, would bear little fruit and multiply United States security concerns in a strategic region.

To put the Latin American drug trade in perspective, is to acknowledge that it is a problem shared by all the nations in the Western Hemisphere. As rising addiction to cocaine continues to ravage American societies, each side can no longer afford to point the acusing finger at the other. The Latin American drug trade is an inter-American phenomenon and the solution will have to be inter-American in nature. As each nation comes to terms with its own addict population, casting the blame on each other will not be an effective method of dealing with what is likely to become a deteriorating situation.

Although the response in Latin America has been slow, Latin American elitists have begun to regard drug trafficking increasingly as a dangerous development that merits greater attention. In August 1984, the government of Ecuador hosted a meeting of official representatives from Bolivia, Colombia, Nicaragua, Panama, Peru, and Venezuela. The narcotics trade was condemned—a significant change in elite attitudes concerning the problem. A disappointing element about the meeting was that at least two of the governments that participated, Nicaragua and Panama, had high-ranking government officials involved in the drug trade.

There were other efforts to move against the drug trade in Latin America in the early 1980s. In 1984, the production of cannabis in Colombia was largely eliminated. In Mexico, inroads were made into reducing heroin production. Despite these efforts, the Latin American drug trade continued to grow because it appeared that when drug production and exportation were eliminated in one region they commenced and/or developed in another. In a sense, the gains against the drug trade in one country have often led to expansion elsewhere.

## LOOKING FOR SOLUTIONS

A number of solutions have been offered to deal with the Latin American drug trade. However, there appear to be differences in the perception of who is to blame; should measures be taken against the supply or the demand side? The Reagan administration placed an emphasis on the supply side, seeking to pressure Latin American governments to be more aggressive and to rely on interdiction along United States borders. The South Florida Task Force made use of radar aircraft, helicopters and custom-made pursuit craft, seeking to act as a highly visible deterrent to the inflow of drugs. While the high-tech "Miami Vice" approach made southern Florida's border more difficult to pierce, the traffic shifted into neighboring states such as Alabama and Texas.

Interdiction has also been influenced by the changing nature of the Latin American drug trade. As the domestic marijuana crop grew to be the second largest cash crop behind corn in the United States, the demand for imported cannabis declined. At the same time, cocaine proved to be an easier drug to smuggle, considering that marijuana had to be smuggled in large bales. James Lieber noted the differences between transport of both drugs: "A ton of marijuana had the same market value as a kilogram of cocaine, but one was the size of a car, the other no bigger than a two-pound bag of sugar."[12] Simply stated, marijuana presented a much simpler target for drug enforcement officials than cocaine. This is not to say, however, that marijuana smuggling had vanished. Instead, some marijuana traders opted to trade in cocaine which was easier to smuggle while others stayed with the first commodity. Demand for foreign marijuana also decreased due to greater productivity in the United States.

The interdiction approach has also led to the development of a symbiotic relationship between narcotics agents and the smugglers. As Lieber observed:

> The smugglers understand Washington's need to see a steady rising number of arrests and confiscations. As a result, a smuggler sends into the country not less cocaine but more—divided among several boats, one of which the smuggler considers expendable. If the police capture the decoy, they get some cocaine, a boat, a crew, statistics, and arrests.[13]

Other approaches have included drug prevention education (demand-side), alternative crops (supply-side), and the sending of antinarcotic advisory teams to Latin America and the Caribbean (supply-side). For varying reasons, these have had only limited success. Though the Reagan administration advocated drug prevention education, it has yet to devote substantial funding for this approach due to budgetary constraints and the emphasis placed on the costly interdiction strategy. The Department of Education's budget for programs to combat drug abuse was reduced from $14 million in 1981 to $2.9 million in 1985. While the emphasis has been on interdiction, the Reagan administration has sought, to its credit, to maintain a high profile on the issue. Nancy Reagan, in particular, sought to draw more attention to the dangers of drug addiction as mirrored in her television program, "Chemical People." Prevention, however cannot help those already dependent and as long they remain so, a substantial domestic market continues to stimulate demand that drug traders seek to meet.

In the war on drugs in Latin America, there will be no quick victories and the approach of North and South American governments will have to be inclusive of supply-side and demand-side strategies. Legalizing cocaine, marijuana, and heroin, a frequently advocated demand-side approach is clearly not a solution which can reduce addict populations or stop societal deterioration. In Amsterdam, one of the Netherlands' largest cities, an exceedingly liberal approach to drug use has prevailed since the 1970s. In that European city, heroin and cocaine are readily available to an expanding addict population. The result is as Rosemary Brady observed:

For a city of 750,000 the crime file is indeed frightening. Muggings have increased sevenfold since hard drugs first gripped the city in the early 1970s. Last year (1983) police recorded some 2,500 robberies, 50,000 pickpocketings and other petty thefts, 147 rapes and assaults and 24 murders. The reported rapes and assaults may represent just 20 percent of the total, police guess. The city's estimated 14,000 hard drug users are blamed for 90 percent of the crimes.[14]

In the Dutch situation it was also noted that tolerance and liberal drug laws attracted more foreign addicts to Amsterdam. Liberalization simply opened a Pandora's box of problems that has taxed even the patience of the Dutch, traditionally one of Europe's most tolerant peoples. What would this approach do in the United States? What would it do in Latin America? It is doubtful the outcome would be positive.

Whatever the approach, success or failure will depend on political factors related to the capacity of both United States and Latin American nations in containing the drug-insurgency nexus and dealing with the tradition of cultivating coca and marijuana in variouus regions. There is, therefore, a direct link between drug control and improvements in political and economic infrastructures. It is essential that Latin American governments establish their authority in growing and trafficking areas.[15] Without control, reforms mean nothing. At the same time, coercive measures are not the sole policy option: it is also crucial that income alternatives be created for farmers of illicit crops. Seeking to crush the drug trade by military means would undoubtedly provoke substantial peasant unrest, something the governments in Bolivia and Peru would have difficulties in contending with. Moreover, it is in those nations that the growers are politically powerful and well-organized. The attitudes of Latin American elitists, however, are changing and the need to take a more aggressive stance is gradually gaining ground. For the United States, therefore, it is crucial that supply-side solutions be advanced simultaneously with comprehensive demand-side remedies. The United States domestic front cannot be ignored: it is not diplomatic to criticize others while one's own house is not in order.

Most of the issues raised in this chapter will be examined in greater detail in the following chapters. Above all, one element which figures most importantly throughout is the prominence of the political nature of the Latin American drug trade. The political side has become dominant, effecting United States—Latin American and inter-Latin American relations. In some cases, the very survival of the government has become part of the tangled politics of the drug trade. The drug-insurgency nexus, with its outside linkages, clearly has become a growing concern and it is crucial to develop a better comprehension of the problem, exploring the consequences as well as the solutions.

## NOTES

1. Brian Freemantle, *The Fix: Inside the World Drug Trade* (New York: Tom Doherty Associates, Inc., 1986) and James Mills, *The Underground Empire: Where Crime and Governments Embrace* (Garden City, New York: Doubleday & Company, Inc., 1986). On the social science one study that was valuable was Jonathan F. Galloway and Maria Velez de Berliner, "The Worldwide Illegal Cocaine Industry," a paper presented at the 28th Annual Convention of the International Studies Association, Washington, D.C., April 15–18, 1987.

2. Figures are from the *National Narcotics Intelligence Consumers Committee* (NNICC); Rensselaer W. Lee III, "The Latin American Drug Connection," *Foreign Policy*, 61 (Winter 1985–86): 146; and James Lieber, "Coping with Cocaine," *The Atlantic Monthly*, January 1986: 39.

3. "What is our Drug Problem? Forum," *Harper's*, December 1985, p. 41.

4. James Lieber, "Coping with Cocaine," *The Atlantic Monthly*, January 1986, p. 39.

5. Jackson Diehl, "Surge in Cocaine Traffic Sparks Venezuelan Antidrug Campaign," *Washington Post*, November 22, 1984: p. 8.

6. Quoted in Angelia Herrin, "Latins Divert Land; Plant Coca, Not Corn." *Journal of Commerce*, October 18, 1985, p. 4. Also see Doreen Gillespie, "Peru Agriculture Minister Resigns," *Financial Times*, January 8, 1986, p. 4.

7. Organization of American States, "Socio-Economic Studies for the Inter-American Specialized Conference in Drug Traffic," Inter-American Specialized Conference of Traffic in Narcotic Drugs, General Secretariat of the Organization of American States, Washington, D.C., April 22, 1986, p. 21.

8. R. W. Lee, Jr., "The Latin American Drug Connection," *Foreign Policy* 61 (Winter 1985–86), pp. 142–143.

9. *Latin America Regional Reports Andean*, June 24, 1983, pp. 7–8.

10. Riordan Roett, "Peru: The Message from García," *Foreign Affairs* 61, 2 (1985), p. 251.

11. Quoted in Lee, "The Latin American Drug Connection," *Foreign Policy* 61 (Winter 1985–86), p. 144.

12. James Lieber, "Coping with Cocaine," *The Atlantic Monthly*, January 1986, p. 43.

13. Ibid, pp. 43–44.

14. Rosemary Brady, "In Dutch," *Forbes*, February 27, 1984, p. 46.

15. R. W. Lee, Jr., "The Latin American Drug Connection," *Foreign Policy* 61 (Winter 1985–86), pp. 158–159.

# 2

# The Historical Perspective: The Incas' Revenge?

## INTRODUCTION

There was nothing pleasant about the Spanish conquest of the New World. It was generally a short, brutish series of invasions conducted by expeditions of driven and ruthless men in search of wealth.[1] The native peoples of the Western Hemisphere, the Arawaks, Chibchas, Mayas, and Aztecs, were militarily defeated and their civilizations destroyed by the combined pressures of internal byzantine politics, disasters on the battlefield, and widespread epidemics caused by diseases introduced by the newcomers.[2]

One of the last major Indian civilizations to fall was that of the Incas, who presided over a sizeable empire that stretched throughout the Andes with present day Peru at the center. In 1532, Francisco Pizarro set out to conquer the Incas, lured by the fabled golden treasures of the Indian empire. By 1533, the Spanish had conquered the core of Inca lands, decimated the population and put many of the survivors to work in the mines. The Incas, however, were not entirely overcome until 1537 when a significant Indian revolt was crushed and a neo-Inca state survived until 1572 in the mountain refuge of Vilcabamba. The Spanish had come to stay, forever changing the Inca's world: in the very lands where they had been the masters, they became the conquered race. Although a few other Indian revolts occurred, the Incas had lost their world, becoming a subclass in a European-dominated Latin American society.

In the twentieth century, well over 400 years since the Spanish conquest, it appears that the Incas may at long last be extracting their revenge on Western civilization through the Latin American drug trade, largely dominated by cocaine, but including marijuana and heroin. Paradoxically, the same technological superiority that allowed the Europeans to subjugate the peoples of the New World, are now helping to facilitate both the production and transportation of illegal drugs that have growing addict populations in North and South America as well as in the Caribbean. At long last, a weapon has emerged to tear at the core of the Europeans' world (North Americans are included in this term), to unravel their society and to apply pressure to their political systems.

The purpose of this chapter is to examine the historical roots of cocaine, emphasizing that the cultivation of coca, the plant from which the drug is extracted, forms a traditional and central element of the South American Indian's world. A lesser focus of this chapter is directed at defining marijuana (also referred to as *ganja*) and heroin. This approach is justified by the overwhelming dominance of cocaine in the Latin American drug trade in total terms vis-à-vis the smaller, yet significant amounts of marijuana and heroin.

## FROM COCA TO COCAINE

No one knows exactly when the first coca leaf was cultivated in South America, though it is likely to have been roughly as early as 1800 B.C., the period when ceremonial organization clearly emerged in the Andean settlements.[3] From that time forward, coca was grown alongside other crops such as manioc, peanut, sweet potato , tree tomato, and pineapple. The rough terrain of the high Andean ridges, especially on the eastern slopes by the Amazonian headwaters, has traditionally proven to be the most fertile for coca production. This region, referred to as the "Eyebrow of the Jungle" is characterized by chasms and valleys and touches present-day Bolivia, Brazil, Colombia, Ecuador, and Peru.

Diverse kinds of coca (*Erythroxylum coca*) were cultivated well before the Spanish conquest. The plants can be harvested as early as eighteen months after planting, and can be harvested from three to four times annually for up to twenty years.[4] From the evidence that exists, it is likely that in the days of the Inca Empire, consumption was integral to many religious and nonreligious ceremonies and was used as a form of tribute within the Imperial system.[5] The wide-ranging dimensions of coca in the Indian world were noted by James Dunkerly:

Coca is frequently exchanged between families or groups as part of minka'a or ayni, systems of reciprocal labour or favours, and still plays a very important role in ritual and recreation. It is used mostly as a stimulant at work but viewed equally widely as a medicine giving protection against the cold and dulling hunger; it also possesses the qualities of an aphrodisiac although these are less marked than in cocaine. The coca leaf is continually masticated and held in the cheek in a ball, its chemical properties being released by the addition of a small amount of alkaline substance (llujta or tocra), usually ash from vegetables.[6]

Three Bolivian writers, René Bascopé Aspiazu and the father and son team of Amando Canelas Orellana and Juan Carlos Canelas Zannier have extensively covered the subject of coca use in Bolivian society.[7] The latter authors noted and the former concurred that "coca is an essential, integral factor in the life of the *campesino*; it constitutes a mediating element with the everyday supernatural, to help calm the gods and put one in favor with them."[8] Similar studies have found the same to be true in Peru, past and present.[9]

Coca's use did not continue without attempts to control it by both Old and New World governments. The first Spanish administrators initially taxed it, feeling that if the Indians prized it, then it would have some value. This, however, was not successful and after several attempts at banning coca, the Spanish began using it as a portion of the monthly salaries of Indian laborers, a practice that survived into the twentieth century.[10]

Widespread coca use also became a problem for the Spanish. Despite strong legislation passed by Philip II of Spain in 1560, 1563, and 1569 against the use of the leaf, coca use continued in the New World, spreading into the ranks of the Iberian ruling class. As William D. Montalbano noted: "By 1617, the chewing of coca leaves were so common among members of the Spanish clergy in the colonies that a synod in Bogota denounced it as 'the most efficient instrument for communication with the devil' "[11] Coca use, however, did not spread to Europe on a grand scale due to its being regarded, in a sense, as an Indian cultural more and not fitting for the civilized Spanish.

During the colonial period, therefore, coca production and use continued. Its prosperity as a commodity, however, was linked to the major exports of what were later to become the nation-states of Peru and Bolivia. These commodities were silver, tin and other ores, mined under usually difficult and physically demanding conditions. As these exports were influenced by price fluctuations in the international marketplace, coca production was also affected by the ups and downs of the market. The cycles of boom and bust that afflicted the mining industries, also afflicted the coca industry, legal and illegal, determining expansion and contraction of cultivation, capital invested and employment. Despite the disruptive period during the Latin American wars of independence against Spain, the symbiotic relationship between coca production and mineral exportation remained constant, existing primarily in Bolivia and, to a lesser extent, in Peru.

In Bolivia, coca production initially flourished or slumped in relation to the fortunes in the silver industry. During the colonial era, coca production probably never exceeded 4,000 tons a year and at least a third of it was consumed in the major mining center of Potosi.[12] Primary cultivation areas were in the Yungas region around what became the Bolivian capital of La Paz. Two major townships dominated, being Coripata and Chulumani. The latter was dominated by indigenous communities, who were oriented towards small-scale cultivation. Much of their produce went to local use. In Coripata, however, large haciendas predominated and were oriented towards commercial production.

As Bolivia's economy shifted from an emphasis on silver to tin in the late 1800s and early 1900s, Coripata's haciendas benefitted and expanded in size. It was only later in the 1950s when agrarian reforms were undertaken that production was converted to small-scale holdings: the new minifundistas acquired plots of land that were fertile but too small to allow viable commercial operations.[13] The result was as Dunkerly noted, "Production certainly fell and trading often took the form of barter."[14] It was not until the new boom in the seventies, stimulated by outside demand that coca production for conversion into cocaine was revitalized, and large-scale operations for cultivation were re-introduced.

While legal production continued in a long and somewhat unbroken pattern in Bolivia, there was resistance to it elsewhere in post-Imperial Latin America. Once again a cultural element must be considered: in the region's societies, European cultural mores were held above all others. The cultural emphasis was white, Catholic, and Western. For non-Europeans, assimilation of those values was crucial for any upward social mobility. This situation was the most pronounced in Peru, Ecuador, and Colombia, nations with sizeable Indian populations. It was far less a concern in Argentina and Chile which had small or non-existent Indian populations. Along these lines, coca chewing was frowned upon as something which was a distinctively Indian tradition.

In Peru, the upper class in the nineteenth century was largely of European, mainly Spanish descent. The Indian population was clearly looked down upon and lived extensively outside of the major urban areas such as Lima. Most habits perceived as Indian were frowned on as backward, linked to a nonprogressive past. As Peru developed as a nation-state, the Indians were expected to assimilate European civilization as much as possible although that in itself did not guarantee acceptance or immediate upward social mobility. This situation was noted by Henry E. Dobyns and Paul L. Doughty: "Officers took particular pride in the ability of the army to stop conscripts from chewing coca, a major symbol of the Indian abhorred by cigarette-smoking middle-class urbanites."[15]

Peru was not the only nation to attempt a curbing of coca use. There have been many attempts and as many failures as coca always managed to survive. The presidents and prime ministers of contemporary governments are clearly not the first to contend with the problem. They are in the company of the early Spaniards, nineteenth century Latin American governments and militaries, and even an earlier generation of twentieth century leaders, such as Colombian President Mariano Ospina, who in 1947 banned the cultivation, sale, and consumption of coca (and marijuana). Strongly opposed to coca, the Colombian head of state rescinded his own law, after what he ruefully called "a true tempest." [16] For many Latin Americans, especially Andean Indians, coca continues to have a central role in culture and society and henceforth, there has remained through several centuries, deep-rooted opposition to its disuse. An effective banning of coca, according to anthropologist Catherine Allen, would threaten to disrupt the Indian's spiritual balance, as a core element would be removed, but nothing new would be substituted. [17]

While coca has been around for several centuries, cocaine is a relatively new substance. It was only in the 1860s that European scientists succeeded in extracting the cocaine alkaloid from the coca plant. The drug soon became available in pure form and was in heavy demand in the medical world as a painkiller and anesthetic. As cocaine was experimented upon in Europe and the United States in the late 1800s, it gradually created a need for greater supply. In time, a legal pharmaceutical industry developed in a number of Latin American nations to meet the demand. By the 1920s, cocaine was being produced in large quantities for the first time. As this occurred, more research on the narcotic revealed a number of negative side-effects, such as addiction, and controls were implemented. While cocaine or the coca plant continued to have a now limited role in the medical world, the substance existed for the illegal side of smuggling and use in Europe and the United States.

What exactly is cocaine? Cocaine is in the same chemical family as nicotine, caffeine, and morphine. It is extracted from the coca plant, which is cultivated chiefly in South America. The extract is heated with hydrochloric acid and the result is cocaine hydrochloride, a form of salt often mixed with various adulterants. This byproduct is the mainstay of the trade, as it is water-soluble making it easy to take in several different ways. [18] Lieber noted:

The cocaine molecule resembles the local anesthetics procaine (Novacain) and lidocaine (Xylocaine) in structure. All three consist of an amino group with a focal nitrogen atom and a six-carbon ring that facilitates solubility in fatty tissue (such as the tissue of the brain). Although cocaine is itself a local anesthetic, it is also a stimulant of the central nervous system—possibly the most potent in nature. [19]

Lieber also described the effect of cocaine on the senses: "The 'rush'—the sense of euphoric excitement—reported by users of the drug probably comes from the activation of nerve cells in the brain that release a chemical messenger, or neurotransmitter, called dopamine, which is associated with pleasure, alertness, and motor control."[20] The sensation, according to one psychiatrist, is that the brain is tricked into feeling as though it had been "totally supplied with food and sex."[21] While there is the euphoric effect, other results are excitation, increased alertness, insomnia, loss of appetite, increased heart rate, increased respiration, and increased blood pressure.[22] Repeated use of cocaine can result in chronic fatigue, convulsions, depression, irritability, loss of sex drive, memory problems, nasal bleeding, paranoia, severe headaches, increased body temperature, and death (due to, among other causes, cardiac arrhythmias or cerebrovascular accidents).[23]

There are two major types of cocaine usage. The first is intranasally, and the absorption of the drug is relatively slow, beginning in minutes. As Drs. William H. Anderson and Karen R. Reeves noted of this usage: "It produces a sense of clarity of thought, efficiency and energetic health" and "... this pattern shows decreasing intervals between usages, and eventual decline of health and social competence."[24] The second type of usage is freebasing of crack, a concentrated form of cocaine. Smoked in a pipe, this substance is rapidly absorbed into the bloodstream from the lungs and produces a much more intense sensation of pleasure for a shorter timespan. Freebasing is highly addictive in a short period of time, while intranasal usage can be practiced over a duration of years.

In animal studies conducted by Michael A. Bozarth and Roy A. Wise of Montreal, the effects of heroin and cocaine were compared on rats. The rodents were allowed unlimited access to each drug and after two weeks, 70 percent of the rats taking cocaine were dead, while 90 percent of those that self-administered heroin were alive, indicating that the toxic effect of cocaine greatly exceeds that of heroin.[25] Cocaine stimulates the area of the brain through which all pleasure signals are directed and in the Montreal study, most of the rats involved refused opportunities to eat or breed, dying within a few weeks. Although this was a single experiment conducted on rats, it does raise questions about the drug's impact on humans. One must wonder whether the human brain possesses a similar "pleasure gate" as that of a rat. If this is likely, then considerable danger clearly exists with cocaine usage. Furthermore, the drug is relatively unpredictable. Dr. Mark Gold, the director of research at Fair Oaks Hospital in New Jersey, noted: We have no way of predicting who'll die from the drug and who won't. It could be a regular user or it could be a first-time user."

Considering the power of cocaine, its ability to provide pleasure and its addictiveness, it has indeed grown into a major problem in the later decades of the twentieth century. As the Spaniards and Latin American governments were unable to halt the consumption of coca, which had a place in the Indians' culture, Western governments appear to have an equally dismal record in the eradication of cocaine and must also contend with what has been called a "counterculture" of those lured into the world of drug consumption. The situation is made no better as the production of cocaine is neither highly sophisticated nor very costly: the leaf is placed in a tub, mixed with diluted sulphuric acid, trodden into a paste; alcohol is added, the syrup is syphoned off, left to solidify, and the cocaine is then washed in either ether or acetone. The product is then smuggled through Latin America and the Caribbean to the lucrative markets of North America.

Two other offshoots of the coca plant that are produced along similar lines are "basuco" and "crack," both, as already noted, highly addictive. Basuco is coca base, the penultimate stage of processing coca leaves into cocaine. A brown powder, usually smoked in a mixture of tobacco, it produces an instant high that lasts for five minutes and leaves the smoker with a strong craving for more. The danger of basuco is that it has not been purified as has cocaine: it carries residues of kerosene, leaded gasoline, sulphuric acid, and potassium permanganate that can cause irreversible damage to the liver, lungs, and brain.[26]

In contrast to basuco, crack is usually cocaine hydrochloride that has been refined backwards to its former state, coca base, and smoked by itself in a pipe. Crack is often purer than basuco, lacking impurities and producing a short-lived high almost instantaneously. The major market for this narcotic has been the United States, while basuco has been limited to Latin America. Both appear to have been introduced in sizeable quantities in the early 1980s.

## THE SISTERS: MARIJUANA AND HEROIN

Marijuana and heroin were not part of the Inca world, yet they are an important part of the Latin American drug trade. The former is largely produced in the Caribbean, Mexico, and Colombia (as well as in the United States) and the latter is limited to Mexico. Heroin was long thought to be the drug of the inner city poor and marijuana appears to have permeated all levels of North American society as well as being used in the Caribbean Basin as in Jamaica, Belize, Colombia, and Mexico. These two drugs are the sisters, perhaps less attractive, yet related to cocaine. Moreover, they have been in vogue at earlier periods and have lost considerable ground to their better endowed sister.

Heroin is a white, odorless, highly addictive narcotic derived from morphine. Its chemical name is diamorphine hydrochloride and it is obtained from the opium poppy. Gum is tapped from the incised poppy head after the petals have fallen. That gum is prepared and treated so that the morphine base can be chemically extracted from it. From that point, the base is mixed with acetic anhydride and converted to heroin base (diacetyl morphine) and hence into a soluable salt, diamorphine hydrochloride. Ten kilos of opium convert into approximately 1.1 kilos of heroin, making access to large amounts of poppy plants essential for commercial operations. Roger Lewis noted other characteristics of the opium plant: "With its high price, high yield per acre, labour-intensive nature and inaccessibility on high, rugged, hard-to-control terrain, opium is a tempting cash crop for improverished tribal peoples who have successfully integrated the poppy into their domestic economy and culture."[27] In many respects, opium functions in a similar fashion to coca in parts of Asia and in the Middle East. As a fairly recently introduced cash crop, cultivation in Mexico, does not have as much cultural dimension as it does an economic incentive.

Though it can be smoked or sniffed, heroin is usually administered intravenously. It is sometimes injected with cocaine as "speedballs." Heroin was traditionally regarded as the drug of poor, usually minority, urban dwellers. In the United States it was associated with the unemployed, minority male with little education who often commits crimes to support his habit. B. Hanson noted: "Because of the regular availability of heroin and the structure of the relationship of inner city residents to society, the heroin lifestyle has become firmly established as an alternative lifestyle for youngsters."[28] Heroin use, however, is not limited to the poor inhabitants of the inner city. Its use has extended into the more affluent middle class and not all users become addicts. There appears to be a group of part time users, referred to as "chippers."

In the 1980s, another group of heroin users have emerged. They are usually middle class and turn to heroin as a result of cocaine usage. One government study noted: "In order to counteract the effects of heavy cocaine use, many begin to use heroin intranasally, and eventually became addicted to the drug."[29] The scope of the problem was outlined by Dr. Forest Tennant, director of a number of drug abuse clinics in California: "I'm treating people who pay their union dues, go to the PTA, take their kids to Little League. We've even got a program for executives."[30]

While heroin has had a somewhat limited market in North America and has been traditionally supplied from non-Latin American areas such as Turkey and Southeast Asia, marijuana has clearly penetrated the United States market. Marijuana has had global usage. In China, well before the birth of Christ, its use was a respected part of medical practice in the treatment of glaucoma and hypertension. Marijuana has also been used for centuries in India and it was the movement of Indians to the Caribbean in the early 1800s that introduced its usage to the Western Hemishere. Today, it has grown to be the second largest cash crop in the United States and most likely the largest in Jamaica and Belize, while production does not lag too far behind in Mexico. Production in Colombia, once a major exporter, has declined vis-à-vis the other producers due to a combination of government campaigns against its use and cultivation, the comparative easiness of transporting cocaine, and its relative unimportance in most South American cultures. Only in Jamaica and other Caribbean nations does marijuana, which is usually referred to as *ganja*, have a significant role with certain societal groups such as the Rastafarians (also called Rastas).[31]

What exactly is marijuana? Simply stated, it is dried leaves and flowering tops of the pistillate hemp plant. This plant yields cannabinoids, which are smoked in cigarettes for an intoxicating effect. Related to marijuana is hashish, the unadulterated resin from the flowering tops of the female hemp plant (*Cannabis Sativa*). It can be smoked, chewed or drunk. Although marijuana can cause addiction, its negative impact is nowhere as lethal as cocaine or, for that matter, heroin. According to the 1982 National Survey on Drug Abuse, 23 percent of 16-and 17-year-olds, 8 percent of 14-and 15-year-olds, and 2 percent of 12-and 13-year-olds used marijuana at least once per month.[32] Unlike cocaine and heroin, it has almost become part of the mainstream of United States life in the relatively short fifteen to twenty years that it has been used in this country. People can "graduate" from marijuana to cocaine. While marijuana use is not as lethal, the effects are, tragically, pervasive, insidious, and ultimately cause irreversible problems in a user's ability to think. The same can be said for hashish and tetrahydrocannabinol (T.H.C.) powerful derivatives of cannabis.

One of the longstanding arguments about marijuana has been that it is less harmful to the user than is tobacco. However, scientific evidence has demonstrated that assumption to be erroneous. Though both are eventually harmful to the user, tobacco is usually filtered and tobacco smoke is not as deeply inhaled as the unfiltered marijuana. Marijuana is more deeply inhaled, not filtered, and held in the lungs longer than tobacco smoke. The American Lung Association has noted that marijuana smoking harms the lungs and may result in lung cancer, emphysema, and bronchitis.[33] It is also fat-soluble and after inhaling, its effects can be started in the brain, causing alternations in behavior, such as lassitude, torpor, and memory problems.

## THE SMUGGLING TRADITION

The Latin American drug trade has become a viable commercial enterprise worth over $100 billion annually due to the tradition of smuggling in the Americas. Craig Van Grasstek noted: "The demands of mercantilism subjected the Spanish Empire to a series of market distortions that would have given Milton Friedman apoplectic fits, and the eminently practical Creoles of Spanish America responded by smuggling. As in the colonies of British North America, cries for economic freedom helped to fuel the wars of independence."[34] This is especially true in the Caribbean, where it has been a form of economic endeavor dating back to the first years that the Spanish arrived and other European nations sought to expand their trade in the region. In South America, the Colombians have had centuries of smuggling cattle and other contraband across the Venezuelan frontier and the same could be said region-wide of other nationalities. The development of an inter-American drug trade in the late twentieth century, therefore, is no major departure on practices of the past. The commodity is relatively new, but the actual smuggling old.

The tradition of smuggling in the Americas dates back to the Spanish and Portuguese empires. In the 1500s and 1600s, Spain and Portugal sought to develop empires based on the concept of mercantilism. In essence, the colonies existed for the benefit of the mother country. Therefore, all trade was with, and for, the profit of the mother country. The colony would send its natural resources to the mother country, which would produce certain goods and then re-export them back to the colonies, but at higher prices. In the cases of gold and silver, the mother country's coffers were enhanced and revenues from trade helped maintain defense costs against other European interlopers and the bureacracy required to administer an overseas empire.

Smuggling became the only way for many of the Spanish, and later French, colonies to survive in the seventeenth and eighteenth centuries. Many times, the lines of communications between the colony and metropolitan country were sporadic and the former was left to fend for itself. In doing so, there was a strong temptation to trade with merchants from other countries. This trade was illegal because the colonies were not legally authorized to trade with other nations, and smuggling became a part of life for many colonies and their populations. Gold, skins, food, rum, and guns were traded throughout the Caribbean islands and on the mainland. Though Spanish authorities sought to terminate such activities, the contraband trade often flourished. The major problems confronting colonial authorities were a lack of personnel, poor pay for enforcement personnel so that bribery was relatively easy, and the lack of ships and other equipment required to enforce mercantilist rules for the entire South and Central American areas as well as the Caribbean. For those involved in smuggling, the risks were high, but the rewards were often worth it.

In the twentieth century, smuggling continues to be attractive for those that are willing to take the risks. The problems for enforcement also remain, though the means of transport have varied. Whereas the small, swift ship of the past was one of the smuggler's best means of transport, the airplane has assumed a major role in the Latin American drug trade. One United States government study noted: "The speed, mobility and evasive capabilities of air transport have made it the preferred mode of shipment among Colombian traffickers, and many have built airstrips either near or along the coastlines to permit the fast direct export of cocaine."[35] It was also added that on Colombia's north coast alone, there was over 150 clandestine landing strips and three international airports involved in the illegal trade.[36]

Many nations in Latin America and the Caribbean have found smuggling difficult to control because of difficult financial conditions. The advent of the debt crisis in 1982 and the ongoing dimensions of that crisis has often meant that scarce financial resources are not to be diverted away from national developmental goals to halt the trade in drugs, which also brings an amount of capital back into the economy. In addition, most law enforcement agencies in Latin America and the Caribbean are poorly paid, budgets are not large and prestige is not usually high. The large sums that smugglers can offer enforcement officials at times are more than what is earned in the course of a year in terms of a salary. The continuity between the past and present exists and will continue to exist in the smuggling tradition which has found a new commodity.

## CONCLUSION

The Latin American drug trade is dominated by cocaine and its two lesser sisters, heroin and marijuana. It is big business, incorporates most of the Western Hemisphere and has its roots in various traditions spread across the region. The advent of better communications and the intermingling of peoples has had a major impact in the development of the trade. Along these lines, the smuggling tradition has expanded its scope to deal with one of the "hottest" commodities in the late twentieth century. It is somewhat ironic that what was produced by a civilization and people almost totally eclipsed by the Spanish, has such an impact in the last decades of the twentieth century. Perhaps the Incas have indeed had their revenge on the descendants of the Spanish and other Europeans.

## NOTES

1. Kendall W. Brown noted of the Spanish conquest in one region of Peru: "Spaniards first entered the Arequipa region in 1535, soon after the fall of Cuzco,

as they spread throughout the Andes looting, killing, and enslaving the Indians." In his book, *Bourbons and Brandy: Imperial Reform in Eighteenth-Century Arequipa* (Albuquerque: The University of New Mexico Press, 1986), p. 8. Also see John Hemming, *The Conquest of the Incas* (New York: Harcourt Brace Jovanovich, 1970); Guillermo Cespedes, *Latin America: The Early Years* (New York: Alfred A. Knopf, 1974), pp. 11–23; and Bernal Diaz, *The Conquest of New Spain* (New York: Penguin Books, 1963, 1975).

2. For the impact of diseases on the New World populations see Alfred W. Crosby, Jr., *The Colombian Exchange: Biological and Cultural Consequences of 1492* (Westport, Connecticut: Greenwood Press, Inc., 1972).

3. Henry E. Dobyns and Paul L. Doughty, *Peru: A Cultural History* (New York: Oxford University Press, 1976), p. 21. Also see Richard T. Martin, "The Role of Coca in the History, Religion, and Medicine of South American Indians," *Economic Botany*, Vol. 24, (1970), pp. 422–438 and Joel H. Hanna and C. A. Hornick, "Use of Coca Leaf in Southern Peru: Adaptation or Addiction," *Bulletin of Narcotics*, Vol. 29, No. 1, (1977), pp. 63–74.

4. President's Commission on Organized Crime, *America's Habit: Drug Abuse, Drug Trafficking, and Organized Crime* (Washington, D.C.: U.S. Government Printing Office, March 1986), p. 29.

5. James Dunkerley, *Rebellion in the Veins: Political Struggle in Bolivia, 1952–1982* (London: Verso Editions, 1984), p. 310.

6. Ibid.

7. René Bascopé Aspiazu, *La veta blanca: Coca y cocaina en Bolivia* (La Paz: Ediciones Aquí, 1982) and Amando Canelas Orellana and Juan Carlos Canelas Zannier, *Bolivia: Coca, Cocaina* (Cochabamba, 1983).

8. Canelas and Canelas, *Bolivia*, p. 95.

9. See C. J. Allen, "To Be Quechua: The Symbolism of Coca Chewing in Peru," *American Ethnologist*, Vol. 8, pp.–157–171 and R. E. Burchard, "Myths of the Sacred Leaf," Masters thesis, University of Indiana, 1976.

10. William D. Montalbano, "Latins Push Belated War on Cocaine," *Los Angeles Times*, December 1, 1985, in *Information Systems Latin America* (ISLA), p. 309.

11. Ibid.

12. James Dunkerley, *Rebellion in the Viens*, p. 311.

13. Ibid.

14. Ibid.

15. Dobyns and Doughty, *Peru*, p. 210.

16. Montalbano, "Latins Push," etc. p. 312.

17. Catherine Allen, "Ritual alcohol and coca use affect social ties," *News from CASA*, April 1986, p. 2A.

18. James Lieber, "Coping with Cocaine," *The Atlantic Monthly*, January 1986, p. 40.

19. Ibid, p. 40.

20. Ibid.

21. The psychiatrist who made this observation was Mark Gold, who directs drug research at Fair Oaks Hospital, in Summit, New Jersey. Quoted in Leiber, "Coping with Cocaine," p. 40.

22. Secretary of Health and Human Services, *Report to Congress: Drug Abuse*

*and Drug Abuse Research* (Washington, D.C.: U.S. Government Printing Office, 1984), p. 108.

23. Drug Enforcement Agency, *Drugs of Abuse* (Washington, D.C.: U.S. Government Printing Office, 1985), p. 40.

24. Jane Gross, "A New, Purified Form of Cocaine Causes Alarm as Abuse Increases," *The New York Times,* November 29, 1985, p. B6.

25. Quoted in Gina Maranto, "Coke: the Random Killer," *Discover,* March 1986, p. 19.

26. Gross, "A New, Purified Form of Cocaine Causes Alarm," p. B6.

27. Roger Lewis, "Serious Business—The Global Heroin Economy," In Anthony Henman, Roger Lewis, and Tim Maylon (editors). *Big Deal: The Politics of the Illicit Drug Business* (London: Pluto Press, 1985), p. 10. Also see J. T. Maher, *Opium and Its Derivatives* (Washington, D.C.: U.S. Government Printing Office, 1980).

28. B. Hanson, *Life with Heroin* (New York: Bill Walton Press, 1985), p. 176.

29. President's Commission on Organized Crime, *America's Habit,* p. 40.

30. *The Los Angeles Times,* January 25, 1985, p. 1.

31. Shelia Kitzinger, "The Rastafarian Brethren of Jamaica," In Michael M. Horowitz (editor). *Peoples and Cultures of the Caribbean: An Anthropological Reader* (Garden City, New York: The Natural History Press, 1971), p. 581.

32. President's Commission on Organized Crime, *America's Habit,* p. 50.

33. Official Statement of the American Lung Association," quoted in *USA Today,* August 9, 1985, p. 8. Other dangers outlined in "Brief sketch of two drugs," *The New Belize,* (June 1986), p. 7.

34. Craig Van Grasstek, "Colombia and Its Billion Dollar 'Other Economy,' " *Journal of Commerce,* November 14, 1983, p. 14.

35. President's Commission on Organized Crime, *America's Habit,* p. 83.

36. Ibid.

# 3

# Colombia:
# The Volcano's Core

## THE VOLCANO'S CORE

It is the purpose of this chapter to examine Colombia's role in the Latin American drug trade. That South American nation is the single most important country in Latin America in terms of exporting cocaine and marijuana to North America. In the analogy of the drug trade being a volcano, Colombia is the core from which the lava erupts. The Colombian drug dealers best known as the "Medellín cartel" and their guerrilla allies in the drug-insurgency nexus have accomplished more than many nation-states throughout history; they have created transnational trade networks, established trading posts, such as Miami and New York City, and when challenged have demonstrated that they are capable of assassinations, bribery of international officials, and full-scale military-style assaults. Colombia has evolved as the core in the Latin American drug trade because of its high level of involvement in the production, processing, and marketing of cocaine, marijuana, and other narcotics. Anthony Senneca of the United States Drug Enforcement Administration has said "The Colombians are pretty much just dope peddlers and they have become the world's experts at it."[1]

Colombia's involvement in United States cocaine trafficking originated with the influx of Cubans to South Florida in the wake of the Castro Revolution in the early 1960s.[2] Elements within the newly transplanted refugee community were part of an organized crime network, referred to as the "Cuban Mafia." North American organized crime groups were active in Cuba during the 1940s and 1950s and it was only natural that domestic "criminal" entrepreneurs would arise. When Fidel Castro and the July 26th Movement came to power in Cuba in 1959, the Cuban mafia, with its North and South American connections, fled to the United States.

The initial Cuban involvement in narcotics arose from the demand generated by members of the transplanted community that used cocaine as a "luxury" drug. The ties to cocaine trafficking organizations in South America, already established in pre-Castro Cuba, were easily tapped. What commenced as a servicing of a social luxury to Florida's Cuban community, expanded rapidly in the mid–1960s as demand in the United States grew and the market's lucrativeness became apparent. The major source for the Cuban drug enterprises were the Colombians. One United States government study noted: "By 1965 Colombians supplied nearly 100 percent of the cocaine moving through the Cuban networks. Colombians refined the drug and Cubans trafficked and distributed it in the United States.[3]

The Cuban-Colombian alliance was highly successful and it quickly became a powerful force in the Latin American drug trade. However, the Colombians desired a larger role. The South Americans were, after all, the producers who worked through Cuban middlemen. The Colombians realized that the profits would be greater without the services and costs of the Cubans, especially if they could develop their own networks. In the late 1960s and early 1970s, the Colombians expanded their operations from production to trafficking. By 1978 the Colombian drug barons had severed all ties with the Cubans and assumed the dominant role they have continued to play in supplying cocaine to the North American market.[4]

There are four major reasons for Colombia's preeminent position in the Latin American drug trade. First and foremost, the South American country benefits from its geopolitical position. It is strategically located between the coca producing nations of Peru and Bolivia and the routes through the Caribbean and Central America that lead to the lucrative North American and European markets. The Colombians purchase the raw material, process it, and market it. Though the Colombian government applied considerable pressure on Colombian production centers, the *narcotraficantes* moved some of their processing out of the country to neighboring regions in eastern Ecuador and western Brazil.

Secondly, South America's vast central forests effectively conceal clandestine processing laboratories and airstrips that facilitate the traffic.[5] The geographical attributes are complemented by reason number three— the strong entrepreneurial skills of the Colombian people and their early involvement in the trade. One study observed: "They have evolved from small, disassociated groups into compartmentalized organizations and are sophisticated and systematized in their approach to trafficking cocaine in the United States."[6] Brian Freemantle indicated that Colombia's "success" in the drug trade is due to "business ability and refining and distribution expertise."[7] The fourth and final factor has been the willingness of certain elements of the Colombian community in the United States to provide access to markets and function as a distributor network for Colombian cocaine.[8]

The involvement of Colombians residing in the United States was made evident in January 1982 when Orlando Galvez, his wife, and two small children were ruthlessly murdered in a hail of gunfire in New York City. Galvez had established a cocaine-dealing business in the borough of Queens and his suppliers in Colombia suspected that he was dealing with another supplier. The Galvez family's liquidation reflected a particularly ruthless dimension about Colombian involvement in the drug trade. While the Cosa Nostra in the United States has usually pursued its vendettas against a single individual, the Colombians have sought to strike at all members of the family and, at times, friends. This was underscored in April 1984 when a Puerto Rican mother Virginia Lopez, then pregnant, her four children, her cousin and her two children and two other young members of the family were shot to death with shotguns. The police felt that this was a Colombian "message" to the Puerto Ricans who were thought to be involved in drug dealing.

The combination of these factors has made Colombia one of the world's major drug producing and exporting nations. Other nations have some of these factors, but not all, the most important being the lack of geopolitical location. Only Mexico in Latin America may come close.

The guiding force behind Colombia's preeminence in the Latin American drug trade has been the so-called Medellín cartel. The cartel allegedly accounts for 80 percent of the cocaine exported to North America, is based in the mountainous city of Medellín, and is dominated by a small core of billionaires. These billionaires include Carlos Lehder Rivas, Jorge Luis Ochoa, and Pablo Escobar. Backed by the capital of the drug trade, the Medellín cartel has, and continues to exert, considerable influence in Colombia. Moreover, the cartel has been one of the major forces in fighting against the 1979 extradition treaty with the United States. In addition, it is highly probable that much of the narcotraficante side of the drug-insurgency nexus has been with the Medellín cartel.

## THE DRUG-INSURGENCY NEXUS

The impact of the drug trade on the nation's political and socioeconomic system has been considerable as it is founded upon an alliance between the drug barons and leftist guerrilla groups. This seemingly strange alliance has been referred to as the *drug-insurgency nexus*. Why is it that leftist guerrillas, who usually espouse a Marxist-Leninist or Maoist revolution, work hand-in-hand with drug dealers, many of whom are politically conservative? Though difficult to prove, it appears that both groups have found working together mutually beneficial. However, before examining these shared benefits, it is important to have some background to Colombia's somewhat violent political tradition that helped shape the drug-insurgency nexus.[9] Of Colombia's political development in the past century, Paul Oquist wrote:

> Between 1946 and 1966, the Republic of Colombia was the scene of one of the most intense and protracted instances of widespread civilian violence in the history of the twentieth century. Known in Colombia simply as *La Violencia*, this social process took at least 200,000 lives, including 112,000 in the 1948–50 period alone.[10]

In response to the extensive deterioration of political stability and the military dictatorship of General Gustavo Rojas Pinilla (1953–57), the nation's two major parties, the Liberals and Conservatives, eventually linked forces into what was known as the National Front. The National Front was a system of power-sharing between the two parties, which guaranteed a role for the opposition. Despite ongoing violence in the 1960s, the country began to stabilize under successive National Front governments. In the 1970 national elections, the National Front candidate, Misael Pastrana Borrero, was almost denied the presidency by the former dictator Rojas Pinilla, who captured 39.1 percent to the Conservative's 40.7 percent. Throughout the 1970s and 1980s, the Liberals and Conservatives dominated the nation's politics despite the emergence of leftist guerrilla forces. In the late 1980s, there has been some movement away from the National Front system of power-sharing to a more clear-cut type of two-party system.

Though it is difficult to make a direct link between *La Violencia* and the drug trade in the 1980s, there is a certain element of continuity in the violence associated with the drug trade. The drug baron-government confrontation has added a new dimension as it has brought into the mixture the drug dealers and guerrillas on one side and the government on the other. In the 1980s, these forces fought a brutal war characterized by the assassinations of judges and high-ranking police officers, the assault on the Ministry of Justice, and the elimination of those leftist guerillas of M–19 associated with the Justice Ministry attack in a pitched battle in downtown Bogota. In the late 1980s, the "war" is far from being concluded as the drug barons still have considerable political, economic and, to a degree, military power. This "counterstate" of drug barons and its left wing terrorist allies embodies the Colombian drug-insurgency nexus.

What are the major guerrilla groups in the late 1980s? There are five well-known leftist organizations, most of which in some sense, were inspired by the Cuban Revolution and who felt that armed revolution was the path to power. These groups are the Colombian Revolutionary Armed Forces (*Fuerezas Armadas Revolucionario de Colombia* or FARC), the pro-Cuban Army of National Liberation (*Ejército de Liberación Nacional* or ELN); the Maoist-oriented Popular Liberation Group (*Ejército Popular de Liberación* or ELP); the Revolutionary Movement of 19th of April (*Movimiento Revolucionario 19 de Abril* or M–19); and a small Trotskyite group called the Workers' Self-Defense (*Autodefensa Obrera* or ADO). Though most of these groups allegedly have linkages to the *narcotraficantes*, the two most politically and militarily significant organizations are the FARC and M–19.

The FARC is the only revolutionary group to have its origins in the civil war between the Liberals and Conservatives which broke out in 1948. Officially established in mid–1966, the FARC was the armed wing of the pro-Soviet Colombian Communist Party (*Partido Comunista Colombiano* or PCC). Though from PCC origins, the new guerrilla force also contained noncommunist elements of older insurgent groups that had been organized in the Southern Guerrilla Bloc. In the late 1980s, it is the largest of the guerrilla movements. The FARC made its appeal along the lines of an improved standard of living and social equality to be brought about by a revolutionary regime based on an ill-defined, yet pro-Soviet Marxist-Leninist ideology. Unlike other guerrilla forces, like the ELN, the FARC had fewer urban intellectuals and lacked ideological sophistication.[11] Largely operating in the countryside where the government was weakly represented, the FARC expanded its organization to around 5,000–8,000 active members and supporters, who covered between twenty-three and twenty-eight "fronts".[12]

While the FARC is an active force in Colombia's southeast, M–19 has been the major operation in the country's northeast, especially along the borders of Venezuela and in certain cities. The M–19 was founded in 1974 by radical members of the National Popular Alliance (*Alianza Nacional Popular* or ANAPO). ANAPO was established in 1961 in opposition to the National Front and as a personal instrument of former dictator Rojas Pinilla.[13] Supported by the urban lower class and traditionally Conservative rural areas, ANAPO presented itself as a populist alternative to the Liberal-Conservative hold of the country's political institutions. Rojas Pinilla's narrow defeat in 1970 caused radical members of ANAPO to claim that the elections had been "stolen" and took to the countryside to begin their insurrection in 1974.

M–19's initial leader was Jaime Bateman, an avowed Marxist-Leninist, who had few compunctions about receiving Cuban assistance. Robert Biles noted of M–19: "It has cooperated in military actions with FARC, but maintains its own staff and areas of operation. There are internal divisions in M–19, particularly between hard and soft lines."[14] The hard line has consistently maintained the need for revolutionary struggle, while the soft line has flirted with the idea of some type of reconciliation with the government and the possibility of participating in the political mainstream. Of its twenty-seven guerrilla fronts, the hard line is dominant in at least five.[15]

The pro-Cuban ELN was the most active guerrilla force in the 1960s, but in the 1970s and 1980s, the FARC and M–19 surpassed it in terms of operations and personnel. It also continued to have enough power to launch a wide-ranging offensive in the summer of 1986 in the departments of Antioquia, Cordoba, Santander, Atlantico, and Cesar.[16]

In November 1982, the government of President Belisario Betancur took measures to end the problem of guerrilla insurgencies by promulgating an amnesty law, covering all combatants. Soon thereafter some 1,500 guerrillas took advantage of the amnesty, while 331 were released from custody.[17] The reaction of guerrilla groups was mixed as M–19 remained largely aloof from the amnesty process, while the FARC cautiously had its members "come in from the cold." Of FARC's twenty-seven guerrilla fronts, only five decided to return to armed struggle and within the pro-Cuban ELN, the "Gerado Valencia Cano" wing accepted Betancur's cease-fire offer. The EPL remained aloof from the amnesty talks and sought to continue fighting.

The amnesty was a bold move by the Betancur government as it sought to end a 35-year-old, constitutionally imposed state of siege. Many of the government's powers to deal with civil disturbances and revolutionary activities were rescinded and previously curtailed civil and political freedoms restored. This changed, however, in March 1984 when the state of siege was reimposed in four departments following a destructive guerrilla assault on the capital of Caqueta Department, Florencia. On April 30, 1984, the government's other major domestic policy stance, a crackdown on the drug industry, resulted in the assassination of the Minister of Justice, Rodrigo Lara Bonilla. In response, the state of siege was reimposed nationwide on a temporary basis. The government was at pains, however, to let the rebel groups involved in truce talks know that the new order was not levelled against them.

While the Betancur administration launched an all-out effort against the drug trade in retaliation to Lara's murder, a cease-fire agreement was negotiated by the government with the FARC, and signed on March 1984. The truce became effective on May 28, with the Colombian leader designating a 43-member National Verification Commission to supervise the agreement.[18] Lara's assassination, however, began to attract attention to possible ties between the drug trade and guerrilla groups. Futhermore, this forced the Colombian public to notice that the "drug problem" which had been perceived as a North American problem, had become a Colombian problem. This is not to argue that the "drug war" did not already exist between the government and the *narcotraficantes*. To the contrary, the government had earlier initiated a struggle against the trade and its antinarcotics teams had been called one of the best in Latin America.[19] The Turbay administration had been active in the late 1970s and early 1980s against the narcotics trade, but the guerrilla problem had demanded priority, sapping resources.

The drug war and the guerrillas were brought together by an escalation of the government's antinarcotics activities, which culminated in the April 1984 raid on what was the world's largest known cocaine production center, a complex of seventeen laboratories at Yuri in the eastern lowlands. Hidden in the jungle, this complex yielded 121,500 kilograms of cocaine and had an estimated value of $1.2 billion. It had forty to sixty employees who were protected by 100 guerrillas from the FARC. This, more than anything else, brought into the open the link between some of the guerrillas and the drug traders. Furthermore, many of the weapons held by the guerrillas were brought from Cuba which purchased the cocaine. The National Defense Minister Matamoros stated: "Everyone knows that the planes leave Colombia with cocaine and that they return with weapons from Cuba."[20]

Lara was a member of a new force in Colombian politics, referred to as "New Liberalism." An offshoot of the Liberal Party, this new group was strongly opposed to the narcotics industry and its corrupting influence. With Betancur's blessing and under Lara's guidance in 1983 and early 1984, judicial reform was undertaken and the extent of drug influence was publicized. In October 1983, it was announced that professional soccer was infiltrated with drug money: six out of fourteen professional clubs in the country were controlled by people linked to the traffic.[21] Lara also said the same of professional bicycling. These accusations and the government's toughening of its antidrug campaign were not taken lightly by the *narcotraficantes*. Striking through congressmen, allegedly financed by drug money, the *capos* made a number of accusations that Lara was himself involved in the drug business.

One of New Liberalism's most visible figures was Luis Carlos Galan. When congressmen linked to the drug barons sought to frame Lara, he stated:

In this moment, the drug traffic knows that its enemy in Colombia is New Liberalism and for that reason it wants to destroy it, it wants to attack it, but we have confronted the vices of clientelism because it was weakening public administration and affecting the political parties, now we are confronting those obscure interests that have been infiltrating the communication media, the very parties, and the social and economic structures of the country.[22]

The government's hardened position, the publicization of the drug mafia activities, judicial reform, and an increased tempo of raids on production facilities all led to a confrontation between Lara and *narco-traficantes*. Following the March 10, 1984 raid, which exposed FARC involvement, the "underground empire struck back." On April 30, 1984 Lara was assassinated on his way home by two hitmen on a motorcycle. One of the assassins was killed by Lara's bodyguards. It was soon revealed that the youthful killer had been contracted by drug barons from Medillín. A five-month investigation disclosed the murder plot was conceived at the country estate of Lara's brother-in-law, Gustavo Restrepo. An inner caucus of drug barons had attended the meeting, contributing $486,000 to arrange the murder.[23] This enraged the government, which intensified efforts against the drug barons. At the same time, Lara's murder mirrored an escalation of violence between opposing forces. This was, unfortunately, only a beginning.

The situation was further complicated by M–19's leader Ospina, who was one of the left's announced candidates for the 1986 presidential elections. Though there had been allegations of M–19 involvement and military-produced evidence of ties to Cuba (drugs-for-guns), Ospina's views on drugs and increased drug-trafficker threats to United States diplomats provided an insight to one line of thinking within the guerrilla camp. In December 1984, the M–19 leader stated:

> May these threats be carried out and may they be carried out in the entire world against the rapacious imperialism that lives at the cost of misery of exploited people.... If the drug-traffickers carried out their threats, it will seem well done to the M–19, and it would be a matter of negotiation if some day those drug-traffickers, who are Colombians also, decided to use their wealth in order to build the country.[24]

Ospina was quickly relieved of the leadership of M–19 because of the statement, yet he provided some insight to the logic behind the drug-insurgency nexus. Simply stated, guerrilla groups like M–19 and elements of the FARC, perceived the drug traffic as a means of generating income for the purchase of arms from Cuba and Nicaragua. Furthermore, the *narcotraficantes'* ability to strike at the state, weakened enforcement measures, which, in turn, meant a greater inflow of drugs into the United States, hence helping undermine the global leader of the imperialist system. Taken to its ultimate conclusion, the weakening of United States imperialism would weaken the dependent-capitalist state in Colombia, which would accelerate the speed of revolutionary change and allow the guerrillas to achieve their long sought victory.

This perception was also reinforced by the substantial military capabilities of the *narcotraficantes* vis-à-vis the guerrillas and the fact that both groups preferred the same terrain—relatively remote jungle outposts that provided cover from the government and allowed the development of communications between base camps and the outside world. Colombia's guerrilla/terrorist groups had initially sought to strike at the *narcotraficantes* through kidnapping. As Freemantle noted of FARC and M–19: "Both recognized the potential of kidnapping relatives of Croesus-rich drug barons as a way of raising limitless money—through ransom—to support themselves and buy arms."[25]

The drug barons, however, proved to be ruthless adversaries, capable of conducting many of the same actions against leading guerrillas and their families. Along these lines it was probable that drug money financed some of the death squads active in the country. One of the best known is MAS, *Muerte à Secuestradores* (Death to Kidnappers), which was created in the early 1980s and was linked to assassinations of left wing party leaders, unionists, intellectuals and students. MAS was established by angry drug barons who had relatives that had been kidnapped or killed by the guerrillas. Organized by Pablo Escobar, one of the major *narcotraficantes*, and Manuel Antonio Garces, 200 leading *capos* (most of the Medellin cartel) attended the founding meeting and agreed to second their most capable bodyguards to a central unified force, MAS. This organization was soon to make itself felt. MAS was also said to have been supported by elements of the armed forces, strongly opposed to communism.

The *narcotraficantes* usually lived in fortress-like homes, had well-equipped private armies, and international connections. They were also exceedingly ruthless in dealing with any serious opposition as reflected by Lara's assassination. Though he was one of the most important officials to be killed, he had not been the first or the last. Considering the strength of the drug barons, it was logical for the guerrillas to make "tactical alliances" which would provide them greater revenues and access to weapons. For the drug barons, the link to the guerrillas provided new small armies for protection, reducing security concerns, except for those from the government. In the trial of Carlos Lehder in late 1987 and early 1988, it was revealed that the members of the Medellín cartel had forged an alliance with M–19, supporting the group with profits from cocaine trafficking. George Jung, one of the witnesses against Lehder and serving fifteen years for importing 660 pounds of cocaine, stated: "They [M–19] were protecting him, helping him consolidate political power in Colombia, and they carried out his executions when asked to."[26] It should also be added that not all guerrilla groups found this arrangement to their liking: while the FARC appeared to have an interest in becoming part of the political mainstream, most elements of the M–19 continued to have ties to the drug-insurgency nexus.

The Colombian government's response to the escalation of hostilities was to declare a state of siege for the entire country "directed against *narcotraficantes*, not the FARC." Raids were carried out against the property of suspected drug barons. In Medellin alone, there were eighty raids that netted weapons, aircraft, radio equipment, and thousands of United States dollars. The government also conducted serial pesticide sprayings of marijuana for the first time in July 1984.

The situation in Colombia had changed as a result of the open challenge posed by the drug-insurgency nexus. The drug traffickers had become too powerful, too conspicuous, and too greedy. They were involved in politics, sports, public works, and in 1982 and 1983 were blatant about their wealth, how they acquired it, and, most importantly, how they wielded their influence. One of the most visible *capos,* Carlos Lehder formed his own neo-Nazi party and had an openly public profile. The link between guerrilla groups seeking to topple the government and the increasingly brash influence of the *narcotraficantes* made a substantial threat to the state and a mockery of the concept of government by law. The New Liberalism movement's public posturing about the drug menace and the reforms initiated by Lara, set the stage for confrontation. Lara's assassination and the government's response led to the next stage of violent escalation. In addition, threats leveled against United States citizens in Colombia only worsened the situation, as Washington grew more supportive of the government.

The main drug merchants were forced to temporarily leave Colombia because of the pressure leveled against them. Neighboring Panama, with its corrupt armed forces (itself involved in the smuggling of drugs and guns) served as a safe haven. This was a situation that the drug traders had not considered and the intensity of the government's pressure resulted in a rethinking of operations in Colombia. What the *narcotraficantes* wanted was to return home without complications. Consequently, they turned to negotiations with the government through the good offices of former Liberal president Alfonso Lopez Michelsen and the Liberal attorney general, Carlos Jiménez Goméz. The former met with Pablo Escobar, Jorge Ochoa, and Rodriguez Gacha, who claimed to represent 80 percent of Colombian cocaine traffickers, in Panama to receive their proposal. That proposal outlined that in exchange for freedom to return to the country and reassume "normal" lives, the *capos* offered to inject $3 billion a year into the economy, dismantle the cocaine "factories," and help rehabilitate addicts.[27]

When the drug lords had moved to Panama they had taken a sizeable amount of their capital, which was reflected by the rise in the value of the dollar on the black market (the black market was 140 pesos and the official rate 100 pesos). As an indication that they were negotiating in good faith, they released some of their funds back into Colombia which caused the dollar to fall in value with the peso: by the end of June one dollar was worth 115 pesos.[28] Despite the evident power of the drug families, the government rejected the offer and Jimenéz and Lopéz Michelsen were strongly criticized. It was felt by the Betancur administration that such recognition as direct talks leading to a negotiated settlement would, in effect, give the drug dealers a status akin to a new sovereign state beyond their control.

The failure of the Panama meeting left the drug barons in a difficult situation. The government showed little inclination of retreating. Lara's assassination had been a tactical error, and increased government pressure was forcing some operations out of Colombia and into remote regions in western Ecuador, Brazil, and Peru. Despite the upheaval for the industry, it was estimated that Colombia's drug exports in 1984 were 500 billion pesos (One United States dollar = 114 pesos). This was roughly equal to $4.4 billion.[29] In addition, the government was unable to capture any major drug figures. As one report noted: "The big traffickers have been able to buy safety, as government officials themselves admit." [30] Many of the major drug dealers quietly returned home and in November 1984, they were linked to the bombing of the bunkerlike United States Embassy in Bogota. They also threatened to kill all leading government figures, including the president and offered contracts for kidnapping the local DEA administrator. Washington responded by having all dependents and children leave Colombia and advised United States citizens not to travel to the South American nation.

What evolved from November 1984 to November 1985 was a war of nerves between the government and the major dealers, while pressure continued against smaller and less-protected operations. The government did make some middle-level arrests and under the stipulations of an extradition treaty with Washington, a number of drug traders awaited court action in Colombia to send them north to be tried in the United States. This treaty had been negotiated between the United States government and the Turbay administration in 1979, but had not been used until Lara's assassination. Its passage had been highly controversial as the question of Colombian nationalism was brought front and center in the debates by the drug dealers through those politicians that they had "bought": if Colombia allowed its nationals to be extradited to the United States, would the United States reciprocate or was it a simple issue of the larger nation pushing its foreign policy objectives (controlling the drug trade) on a weaker nation? Consequently, the treaty had been signed, but not used until the situation intensified in Colombia. By November 1985 most of the cases were pending the attention of the Supreme Court in the Palace of Justice in Bogotá.

## THE ASSAULT ON THE PALACE OF JUSTICE

The drug-insurgency nexus was brought into sharper focus by the bloody November 1985 assault on the Palace of Justice in downtown

Bogotá. The link between M–19 and the drug traders appeared self-evident by the daring nature of the assault, which began when sixty guerrillas rushed the Palace of Justice, a five-story building in downtown Bogotá. After a brief firefight with the guards, the guerrillas overcame the defenders and took almost 400 people hostage, including the President of the Supreme Court, Alfonso Reyes Echandia, and nine supreme court justices. There was an initial announcement that the objective of the attack was "to denounce a government that has betrayed the Colombian people."[31] There was no further explanation that day.

There ensued a 28-hour siege by the armed forces, which was ended by a series of attacks on the Palace of Justice with automatic weapons, 90-millimeter cannons mounted on armored cars, light antitank weapons and explosive charges. In the wake of the final assault, there were some 100 dead and bitter feelings about the government's heavy use of force and M–19's attack. While it initially appeared to be a matter of guerrilla force that attacked a government post, further examination uncovered what is likely to have been a well-coordinated action between the *narcotraficantes* and M–19.

The most shocking element of the entire episode was the number of victims. Ninety-five were killed, including nine judges, one of which was the President of Colombia's Supreme Court. Some of the victims had been deliberately sprayed by rebel fire or had been executed by single shots in the head. Others were caught in crossfires between government security and rebel forces or were killed by the fire that swept through the building during the final assault. At least four justices were executed at point-blank range on Thursday morning when it became apparent that events had turned against them. Despite the use of excessive force to deal with the threat and the relatively high number of casualties, around 300 people were able to escape. Only a few of M–19 members eluded security forces and six members of the guerrilla group's national directorate, including Andres Almarales, were killed.

In the aftermath of M–19's "Operacion Antonio Narino," as it was eventually called, some of the details were made public. It was felt by Colombian intelligence forces that Luis Otero, the man responsible for the planning of the M–19 takeover of the Dominican Embassy in February 1980, organized the assault.[32] One of the motives for the assault was to force the government to re-open negotiations with M–19 that had earlier been broken off in 1984. The military had intensified its efforts against the rebel group, which had sustained high casualties in terms of leadership and personnel. These losses included the group's ideologue Ivan Marina Ospina. Though difficult to actually prove, the assault was probably based on the assumption that Betancur would negotiate and not use force due to his past record of negotiating with the rebel groups and because of the importance of the hostages taken. These proved to be deadly miscalculations.

There was also a darker side to the assault, not directly related to revolutionary ideology. It was highly probable that M–19 and the drug traders had an agreement about attacking the Palace of Justice. There are two major links between the two groups: the guerrillas destroyed drug dealer files and four judges waiting to hear drug-related cases that day were among the victims. One source claimed: "Survivors of the siege claimed that guerrillas quickly burned drug dealers' files and made comments clearly suggesting an alliance."[33] While these factors are important, the testimony of Maria Patino, widow of Justice Alfonso Patino, strengthened the possibility of linkages. She stated that her husband and other Supreme Court justices had received death threats for more than a month prior to the M–19 attack from Colombians due to face extradition proceedings.[34] In the aftermath of the incident, Maria Patino asserted that M–19 guerrillas specifically hunted down her husband and others hearing narcotics cases during the occupation.[35] Another element to support this line of thinking was that security forces had only a month before uncovered a plot by the Ricardo Franco front, a dissident branch of the FARC, to occupy the Palace of Justice.[36] The strong security measures that were then put in force had been lifted only a week before the M–19 attack.

Following the affair and the airing of allegations of linkages to the narcotics trade, Alvaro Fayad, M–19's leader, denied any ties. At the same time, he attacked the "unpopular and scandalous" 1979 extradition treaty with the United States under which Colombians could be sent to the North American country to stand trial for drug-related crimes. Though the treaty had been in place since 1979, it was only in 1984 and 1985 that it was considered for use. Consequently, the day that the judges were to hear submissions challenging the constitutional validity of the extradition treaty with the United States, the guerrillas struck.

There was clearly a ripple effect to the M–19 storming of the Palace of Justice. President Betancur's program of amnesty with the guerrillas was put in jeopardy and there were rumblings within the armed forces that negotiation in this case might provoke a response. Moreover, long-standing charges that the drug-insurgency nexus did not exist and was a propaganda ploy on the part of the United States were largely swept away. The president's firm handling of the affair, which sacrificed the lives of the judges and other victims, widened the ripple effect as more liberal segments of society felt that excessive force had been used instead of negotiation. Conservatives, however, supported the action. An *El Tiempo* editorial commented: "If negotiations had been started . . . Colombians can rest assured that today there would be no state of law and, we believe, no legally based government."[37]

## AFTER THE JUSTICE PALACE

The attack on the Palace of Justice was a spectacular event in the war between the state and the drug-insurgency nexus, but the cost was high and there would be few attempts at a repeat performance. In 1986, Colombia's guerrilla organizations began to extend operations further afield by making linkages with similar groups in neighboring countries. In Ecuador, the *¡Alfaro Vive . . . Carajo!* group emerged and was active in bank robberies. Inside Colombia, there was growing concern as fighting erupted in the region's major oil-producing area and along both the Venezuelan and Ecuadorean borders. By early December 1986, estimated damages from guerrilla attacks was $500 million.[38]

Colombian officials were concerned about the creation of the Batallon America which consisted of M–19, Peru's Tupac Amaro (MTRA), and Ecuador's *¡Alfaro Vive . . . Carajo!*. In January 1987, Colombian President Virgilio Barco and President Leon Febres Cordero of Ecuador met at their common border to discuss drug trafficking, contraband trade, and guerrilla activity. At the same time that Colombia and Ecuador were taking measures against the drug-insurgency nexus, Colombia also co-operated with Brazil and Peru. Though the traffickers have mainly been Colombians, they have been adroit in using international frontiers to escape justice. This situation brought joint actions throughout 1986 on the part of the Brazilian, Colombian, and Peruvian security forces in the Amazonian area.

Not all actions were successful for the Colombian government as the *narcotraficantes* struck back at key officials. On July 31, 1986, Supreme Court Justice Hernando Basquero Borda, who was involved in revising the United States-Colombian extradition treaty of 1979, was murdered. Other important targets were police Colonel Jaime Ramirez Goméz, commander of a number of antidrug campaigns (killed on November 17, 1986) and the editor of *El Espectator*, Guillermo Cano Isaza. The latter was a strong opponent of the drug trade and was assassinated on December 17, 1986. The reign of terror against the government continued into 1987, when Colombia's Ambassador to Hungary, Enrique Parejo Gonzalez, was seriously wounded in an assassination attempt in Budapest on January 13. Parejo had been made ambassador after his appointment as Justice Minister, which had followed that of the assassinated Lara Bonilla. The other major victim was Jaime Paredo Leal, a former presidential candidate and leader of the leftist Patriotic Union Party. He was shot and killed on October 11, 1987 in an apparent reprisal for squabbles between drug bosses and leftist guerrillas in control of local cocaine-growing areas.[39]

One of the most important developments in 1987 was the pursuit and arrest in February of Carlos Lehder, one of the few major drug dealers to be captured and extradited to the United States. It was likely that he had become too much of a visible figure for both the authorities and other *narcotraficantes*. Considering the pressure that the government brought to bear against them, it is possible that they agreed to sacrifice one of their most visible colleagues, Lehder. The pursuit led through the Bahamas and into the jungles of Colombia, finally ending in a courtroom in Jacksonville, where he stood trial in late 1987 and early 1988 on drug charges against the United States. Back in Colombia, the trade still continued. Lehder, however, was one of the last of sixteen Colombians extradited to the United States under the 1979 treaty as the Colombian Supreme Court declared it unconstitutional in June 1987. The *narcotraficantes* have lobbied fiercely against the treaty and subjected Colombian officials to death threats, bribes, and other measures. In addition, many Colombians felt the treaty was a violation of national sovereignty.

While Lehder's downfall was significant, the arrest and escape of Jorge Luis Ochoa, another key figure in the Medellín cartel, opened the way to a set of far more dramatic events. On November 21, 1987 the *narcotraficante* leader was arrested at a checkpoint in western Colombia and sent to a military garrison in Bogotá and later to La Picota jail. Ochoa was arrested on charges of trying to smuggle fighting bulls from Spain into Colombia. At the end of December, Ochoa walked out of La Picota, arm in arm with the warden, released by a low-ranking judge on a habeas corpus plea. The drug baron, wanted for extradition to the United States, then disappeared. While the Barco government was horrified with this development, the United States demonstrated its displeasure by a customs slowdown, which meant that Colombian goods, such as flowers, sat waiting for inspections and perished. In early January, the Barco government indicated that it intended to renew efforts to arrest and extradite Colombia's leading traffickers to face United States criminal charges.

Colombia's internal drug war took another violent twist on January 25, 1988 when Attorney General Carlos M. Hoyos Jimenéz was assassinated along with his two bodyguards on his way to the Medellin airport. Hoyos had spent a week in Medellín examining Ochoa's release from prison. He had ordered an investigation of the two judges and five government officials involved in the incident. The findings from the investigation led to the sacking of the judges and four of the officials. In response, the *narcotraficantes* had declared "total war" on officials who sought to extradite them to the United States. A day later, Hoyos was killed. The Barco government responded by vowing stronger measures against the drug *capos*.

## THE DRUG TRADE'S IMPACT ON COLOMBIA

The impact of the drug trade on Colombia has been profound. It has influenced the nation's political and socioeconomic development: it has been an avenue for upward social mobility for some, a means of financing revolutions for others, and been a major problem for the government as it has permeated even the enforcement agencies and challenged the state's authority in certain regions. In examining the drug trade and Colombia there are a number of factors that must be considered beyond the strictly historical dimension. These include social, financial, and structural elements. Along structural lines, it is important to emphasize that the drug trade is not run by a well-organized, monolithic group, but rather by a number of groups that are far from similar in outlook, motivation, and style.

Mario Arango and Jorge Child, in *Los condenados de la coca* (1986), present a Colombian perspective of the drug trade. The two Colombian economists argue that the United States' "cops-and-robbers" approach is likely to fail as there will always be new traffickers to replace those who are arrested. In addition to the criminal aspect of the drug trade, Arango and Child adroitly note it is one of the few—if not the only—avenues to new wealth in Colombia and that its amorphous nature offers a means of subverting an otherwise rigid class system.[40] The drug trade, therefore, has become a stepping stone for certain elements in society to climb up the ladder and, eventually gain respectability.

These sentiments were echoed by Bruce Bagley, who felt that there were two types of drug dealers in Colombia. One group is the *nouveau riche*—"those people who have used drugs as an avenue of upward mobility, and who, in seeking political protection, have sought to buy political power and social status."[41] Bagley pointed out that they are easily identifiable, flamboyant, and have often veered into the public eye through the media. Carlos Lehder, one of the more flamboyant drug *capos*, fits into this category. Not content with being a major *narcotrafi-cante*, Lehder created a neo-Nazi party, *Movimiento Civico de Liberación Nacional*, that advocated the legalization of marijuana. In time, his high public profile made him an exceedingly visible target for the Colombian authorities. This could be one of the major reasons that he was eventually apprehended in Colombia and extradited to the United States where he was put on trial for drug-related charges. Moreover, many of the second type of drug traders disdained the attention that their industry was receiving and the brazen nature of the *nouveau riche* group.

Bagley characterized the second group as "one that has kept a much lower profile and is far more intertwined with the existing political and social system within the country."[42] This group includes a number of Colombia's oldest families, some of which have lineages dating back to the Conquest. There is no secret about which families have been involved within Colombia: they were identified by Bagley as Davila, the Diaz Granados, and the Castros, all of which are from the departments on the northern coast, especially the Cesar, the Buajira, Magdalena and Bolivaro.[43] Bagley also noted:

The regional and local political systems in these areas are clearly and intimately intertwined with the drug trade. Individuals from these well-known families have served as mayors, senators and governors within the Colombian political system, and they themselves provide political protection to the networks of drug dealers and drug traffickers that have grown up around them. These individuals have not been touched by the recent [1984–1985] campaign in Colombia. They have essentially been able to maintain political protection, whereas the more flamboyant, highly exposed and recently arrived drug dealers have been easy targets and the most forcefully attacked.[44]

The emergence of the two groups has made one group visible and an easier target, while a second and lower profile group remains relatively intact with substantial influence within the nation's political system. In a sense, the drug trade in Colombia has become a hydra, a creature with many heads. Though some of those heads may be severed, others, like the nouveau riche group, are attracted into the industry and make the heads grow back. The older families remain the more experienced heads that are rarely cut off. Operating both within and without the Colombian political system, the drug trade and its domestic side continue to be a part of the nation's socioeconomic development.

Another domestic concern in Colombia is the spread of addiction. In the past, Colombia was not a drug-consuming nation nor was there a long-standing tradition, as there is elsewhere in the Andes, for coca usage as a mild stimulant along the lines of coffee. In the 1980s, however, it became apparent that what had initially been regarded as a "gringo" problem, was becoming a Colombian problem. Part of this was caused by the movement of middle- and upper-class Colombians to the United States for higher education. In many universities, young Colombians, who may have been sheltered at home, were exposed to drug usage. Consumption patterns, beginning in the 1960s and 1970s were then carried back home to eventually grow into a problem in the 1980s. There is also another dimension of the problem that is totally homegrown. The large-scale production of cocaine, like any industry, is susceptible to the ups and downs of international market trends. The recession in the early 1980s probably meant a drop in sales to the United States during that period, which in turn meant that the Colombian dealers were confronted with the problem of a surplus. In the form of *basuco,* a form of coca paste that is smoked rather than inhaled, cocaine was brought into the Colombian market. Sold at lower prices, than refined cocaine used for inhaling and having greater impurities, *basuco* eventually became the drug for the urban poor, especially the younger generations in such places as Medellín.

Another often overlooked result of the drug trade's development in Colombia has been the impact on the country's small Indian population. One of the few small groups to actually cultivate coca in Colombia before it became a major industry, the Indians have found their traditional lifestyles overwhelmed by the entry of the *narcotraficantes* and their allies in the guerrilla movements. Many Indians have gone to work in this sector and materialism, related to new consumption patterns, has made long-term transformations in Indian life. The Indians have also become involved in the violent side of the trade. In late 1985, close to 100 Indians were killed by the FARC in southwestern Colombia.[45] The conflict was purported to be over a dispute within FARC, between the northern organization and the dissident Ricardo Franco group which had the support of the Indians. The dissidents allegedly attempted to assassinate leaders of the Colombian Communist Party, the ideological mentors of FARC. In return, FARC moved against the Ricardo Franco front and its aboriginal allies. The sistuation was further confused by FARC's alliance with local ranchers, who had land occupied by Indians. Ultimately, what evolved was one side composed of FARC, ranchers, and the armed forces against the other side of the Ricardo Franco front, local Indians and M–19 forces in the region. While it appeared to be a struggle based on ideological differences, the strange alliance of FARC, ranchers and the armed forces against the others appeared to be over drug profits. Many of the ranchers had gone over to large-scale coca production in the 1970s, having relationships with both the armed forces and the guerrillas who demanded payoffs. Payoffs were made from the larger agribusinesses as well as the smaller Indian farmers. What sparked the "war within a war" in the southwestern region was " . . . that the Ricardo Franco dissidents broke with FARC'S sixth front over the division in drug profits . . . The story has a certain logic since only money can explain why FARC would renounce an alliance with the Cauca aborigines dating back to the 1960s and tarnish its image as the peasants' champion in land conflicts."[46] The Indians, caught in the middle, therefore, have found their traditional way of life uprooted and, in certain cases, they have been killed.

While considerable attention has been given to the more sensational aspects of the drug-insurgency nexus and the societal problems of addiction and interrelated crime, little has been said about the impact of drug money on the economy. The legal economy has been founded on the traditional export of coffee, which in turn, was affected by fluctuations in price on the world market. In the 1980s, there has been a marked effort to diversify the economy and broaden the range of exports. Though coffee remains the dominant legal export with annual value of close to $2 billion, Colombia also exports coal, oil, flowers, and a growing array of manufactured products. Still, legal exports usually stand at $4 billion yearly, a figure in all likelihood smaller than the export in cocaine, marijuana, and other drugs. Freemantle estimated: "Drugs provide Colombia's biggest source of foreign income, nearly 36 percent of its total gross national product."[47] Moreover, a proportion of the capital earned from the export and domestic sale of drugs has been invested in the country. In cities like Medellín (referred to as the drug capital), many of the beautiful and expensive homes in the surrounding hills are owned by *narcotraficantes* and have helped local construction companies. It is interesting to note that the construction sector's growth rate remained well above the Gross Domestic Product (GDP) growth rate for the country. In 1980, the construction sector expanded at a substantial 9.7 percent, followed by 7.1 percent in 1981, 4.0 percent in 1982 and 5.1 percent in 1983.[48] The corresponding GDP growth rates were 4.2 percent, 2.3 percent and 0.9 percent. The Colombian drug merchants have also donated money to low-income housing, charities, and public facilities.

There is little doubt that there has been some distribution of wealth, which has benefited the lower stratum of society. In addition, cocaine and marijuana production has functioned as an important buffer for the economy, especially the agricultural sector, during times that the market for legal exports have been depressed. This meant that Colombia was in a much better position to weather the economic slowdown of 1979–81 and the recession of 1981. Bagley noted: "About 500,000 Colombians are employed in either the marijuana or cocaine industries, or both, a significant increase from estimates in the early and mid–1970s of 100,000 to 150,000 Colombians. Hence, cocaine and marijuana have had a significant effect on employment during periods when the economy in general has slowed down quite dramatically."[49] Considering that the drug sector has kept the internal economy with a steady flow of capital, the cash flow has meant a relatively strong period of domestic demand that has contributed to the underpinning resilience of the nation's economy.

There have been other negative offshoots for the economy from the development of the narcotics industry. One of the most evident was labor shortages in other parts of the argricultural sector. Large-scale plantation cultivation of bananas, coffee, and sugar increasingly had difficulty in finding pickers and workers as greater money was to be earned with coca and marijuana production. The development of cocaine labs also disrupted and displaced many of the country's indigenous people as they lived in many of the same remote areas that attracted the *narcotraficantes* and guerrillas. In other areas, food production dropped as land was turned to drug cultivation instead of staples, putting pressure on price rises for food. In addition, the financial boom of

the 1970s and the banking system's subsequent overextension were unforeseen outcomes of the inflow of millions of dollars in laundered narcomoney.[50] This inflow of funds also contributed to the rise in inflation
at the close of the seventies and early eighties when the consumer price
index reached 27.5 percent (in 1981).

The massive inflow of drug money, possibly over $500 million an-
nually, eventually had reverberations in the financial sector. Without a
coherent financial policy to deal with this volume of capital, Colombia's
banking sector was swamped. In the 1970s, the government had turned
a blind eye to the laundering of narcodollars, allowing the Bank of the
Republic to have a *"Ventanilla Siniestre"* or Sinister Window, that accepted money from any source with no questions asked.[51] One observer
said of this: "As a result, Colombia became one of the few countries to
have a black market for the dollar below the official price of the dollar."[52]
The financial sector was also plagued with poor loan portfolios: in
1985, the majority of the country's banks had bad or doubtful loans
representing more than double the financial system's total capital and
reserves.[53] Many institutions selflended, others wrote false documentation, and several had facilitated capital flight. At the same time, the
spending patterns of some dealers created problems for banks. Bagley
noted: "At least three major banks in Colombia have closed as a result
of *narcotraficantes* withdrawing funds from them.[54] With the collapse of
a number of financial institutions, the entire sector underwent a difficult
adjustment policy and inflation rose. In the real estate sector in major
cities like Bogotá and Medellín, large amounts of property were bought
with suitcases of cash, which drove land values up and made low-cost
housing more difficult to obtain.

## CONCLUSION

Colombia remains the core of the Latin American drug trade in the
late 1980s, a position that it will probably stay in well into the next
decade and, possibly, the next century. It will continue to have an impact
well beyond its borders. Internally, the drug industry is likely to have
a stabilizing effect on the nation, though violence will remain a factor.
In many respects, the introduction and production of cocaine is much
like that of coffee in the late nineteenth and early twentieth centuries.
Bagley commented: "Parts of the civil wars which were fought in the
latter part of the nineteenth century, particularly the War of 1000 Days
in Colombia, had something to do with the introduction of coffee and
the socioeconomic changes that followed."[55] The point of similarity in
the 1980s is that the current established families are gradually allowing
a newer and wealthier generation of drug dealers and their children into
the upper class. Ultimately, the drug barons are likely to move away

from the drug-insurgency nexus, especially if the guerrillas ever emerge as a serious threat. As the guerrillas currently stand at the close of the 1980s, they remain a largely peripheral force, capable of a degree of disruption, but not total chaos and revolution. Both the guerrillas and the drug traders have used each other, but it is the *capos* that appear to have gained the most.

The drug barons have gradually made inroads to becoming "respectable" and their impact on Colombia's economy remains powerful. With a vast array of contacts, international networks and an entrepreneurial spirit, the Colombians have managed to make the production and export of cocaine a major transnational enterprise or as some would note, a warped aberration of capitalism. Warped or not, the Colombian connection is highly successful and will not disappear at the source. The drug-insurgency nexus is powerful, capable of challenging the state's authority. In the 1980s, the parameters of the relationship were explored, with the state, backed by conservative institutionss like the Catholic church (one of the strongest in Latin America), blatantly responding to overt challenges. While the government could afford to allow a certain leeway with bribery as long as the situation was not obvious, it could not tolerate a direct challenge with drug barons seeking public office, helping guerrillas obtain military equipmnent, and assassinating well-known public officials. The state in Colombia has a long tradition and has the ability to penetrate most parts of society, except for the most remote. This has kept the drug-insurgency nexus in check. Other countries like Bolivia, however, have weaker states and therefore, central authority has been easily challenged. For the drug dealer, Colombia remains home and, as they climb the social ladder, they too will have more to lose from a drug-insurgency nexus that has gone out of control. In a sense, there exists a certain internal control to the relationship between guerrillas and traders that provides certain guidelines as to where the nexus will lead.

## NOTES

1. Quoted in Waren Richey, "Cocaine connection: wealth, violence, drugs and Colombia," *The Christian Science Monitor*, December 20, 1985, p. 8.

2. H. Messick, *Of Grass and Snow* (New York: Bill Walton Press, 1979), p. 24.

3. United States Congress, House Committee Rules and Administration, *Hearings To Create a Select Committee on Narcotics Abuse and Control Before House Committee on Rules and Administration* (Washington, D.C.: 96th Congress, 2nd Session, 1980), p. 70.

4. United States Congress, Senate, *Organized Crime and the Use of Violence: Hearings before the Permanent Subcommittee on Investigations of the Senate Committee on Governmental Affairs* (Washington, D.C.: 96th Congress, 2nd Session, 1980), p. 73.

5. President's Commission on Organized Crime, *America's Habit: Drug Abuse, Drug Trafficking, and Organized Crime* (Washington, D.C.: U.S. Government Printing Press, March 1986), p. 78.

6. Ibid.

7. Brian Freemantle, *The Fix: Inside the World Drug Trade* (New York: Tom Doherty Associates, Inc., 1986), p. 230.

8. President's Commission, *America's Habit*, p. 79.

9. For information on political violence in Colombia see Paul Oquist, *Violence, Conflict and Politics in Colombia* (New York: Academic Press, 1980); Vernon Lee Fluharty, *Dance of the Millions: Military Rule and Social Revolution in Colombia, 1930–1956* (Pittsburgh: University of Pittsburgh Press, 1957); Jorge Gutierrez Anzola, *Violencia y Justicia* (Bogota: Ediciónes Tercer Mundo, 1962); and Robert H. Dix, *The Political Dimensions of Change* (New Haven, Connecticut: Yale University Press, 1967) and by the same author, *The Politics of Colombia* (New York: Praeger Publishers, 1987).

10. Paul Oquist, *Violence, Conflict and Politics in Colombia*, p. xi.

11. J. Mark Ruhl, "The Military," In R. Albert Berry, Ronald G. Hellman, and Maurcicio Solaun (editors). *Politics of Compromise: Coalition Government in Colombia* (New Brunswick, New Jersey: Transaction Press, Inc. 1980), p. 196.

12. President's Commission, *America's Habit*, p. 162. Also see Alan Riding, "Truce Between Colombia and Rebels Is Unraveling," *The New York Times*, August 10, 1987, p. A11.

13. Robert E. Biles, "Colombia." In George E. Delury (editor) *World Encyclopedia of Political Systems and Parties, Volume I* (New York: Facts-On-File Publications, 1983), p. 206 For a more complete study on FARC see Patricia Lara, *Siembra vientos y recogerás tempestades* (Bogotá: Planeta Colombiana Editorial S. A., 1986).

14. Ibid. p. 209.

15. *Latin America Regional Reports Andean*, December 13, 1985, p. 1.

16. Ibid. June 26, 1986, p. 8.

17. *The Latin American Times*, April 15, 1986, p. 4.

18. Ibid.

19. Juan de Onis, "Latin Nations Uniting in War on Cocaine," *The Los Angeles Times*, December 4, 1985.

20. *The New York Times*, March 21, 1984, p. 4.

21. *El Siglo* (Bogota) October 22, 1983, p. 1.

22. *El Espectador* (Bogota), August 29, 1983, p. 1.

23. Freemantle, *The Fix*, p. 216.

24. *El Espectador* (Bogota), December 8, 1984, p. 1.

25. Freemantle, *The Fix*, p. 222.

26. Quoted in Ruth Marcus, "Assault on Cartel Fails to Halt Drugs," *The Washington Post*, February 14, 1988, p. A4.

27. *Latin America Regional Report Andean*, July 27, 1984, p. 4.

28. Ibid.

29. Ibid. December 18, 1986, p. 8.

30. Ibid.

31. Joseph B. Treaster, "Colombian Troops Are Said to Break Courthouse Seige," *The New York Times*, November 8, 1985, p. 1.

32. *Latin America Weekly Report*, November 15, 1985, p. 1.

33. *Business Latin America,* November 13, 1985, p. 366.

34. Peter Nares, "Colombian Guerrillas Drug Connections Crystallize in Shoot-Out," *The Wall Street Journal,* November 15, 1985, p. 31.

35. Ibid.

36. *Latin America Weekly Report,* November 15, 1985, p. 1.

37. Ibid.

38. *Latin America Regional Report Andean,* December 11, 1986, p. 8.

39. Alan Riding, "Colombians Grow Weary of Waging the War on Drugs," *The New York Times,* February 1, 1988, p. A14.

40. *Latin America Regional Report Andean,* December 11, 1986, p. 10.

41. Ibid. p. 8.

42. Bruce Bagley, "The Colombian Connection: The Impact of Drug Traffic on Colombia," in Deborah Pacini and Christine Franquemont (editors) *Coca and Cocaine: Effects on People and Policy in Latin America* (Petersborough, New Hampshire: Transcript Printing Company, 1986), p. 99.

43. Ibid.

44. Ibid.

45. *Latin America Regional Reports Andean,* November 8, 1985, p. 2.

46. Ibid.

47. Freemantle, *The Fix,* p. 211.

48. Inter-American Development Bank, *Economic and Social Progress in Latin America: Natural Resources* (Washington, D.C.: Inter-American Development Bank, 1983 Report), p. 188 and the same author, *Economic and Social Progress in Latin America 1986 Report* (Washington, D.C.: Inter-American Development Bank, 1986 Report), p. 236.

49. Bruce Bagley, "The Colombian Connection," in *Coca and Cocaine,* p. 90.

50. Mario Arango and Jorge Child, *Los condenados de la coca* (Bogota: Tercer Mundo, 1986).

51. Bruce Bagley, "The Colombian Connection," in *Coca and Cocaine,* p. 92.

52. Ibid.

53. *Latin America Regional Report Andean,* July 26, 1985, p. 2.

54. Ibid.

55. Bruce Bagley, "The Colombian Connection," In *Coca and Cocaine,* p. 97.

# 4

# Where Cocaine Is
# King: Bolivia and Peru

## INTRODUCTION

Bolivia and Peru follow Colombia as the most significant forces in the Latin American drug trade. Bolivia and Peru, in fact, together corner the market as producers of coca leaves (between 154,000–188,000 metric tons in 1984), the fundamental raw material for cocaine.[1] Consequently, Columbia is at the volcano's core, but these Andean countries are very close to that position. Without Bolivia and Peru, the cocaine market would be considerably different. The purpose of this chapter is to examine the drug trade in Bolivia and Peru. It is advanced that elements of the drug-insurgency nexus exist in the case of Peru and that there is a strong linkage between crises in national economic development and the spread of the drug trade. The latter is more evident in Bolivia than in Peru.

## WHY BOLIVIA?

Located at the heart of the South American continent, Bolivia is one of the major coca leaf producers in the world (between 46,000–67,000 metric tons in 1987) and a center for the first stages of producing cocaine. It is estimated that the Bolivian coca crop, largely based in the eastern part of the country, yields $3 billion per annum.[2] Roughly five tons of coca paste are sent abroad weekly, most of it headed for the United States through Colombia where it is processed. Of total earnings, an estimated $600 million return to Bolivia where it eventually trickles down from the wealthy drug barons to corrupt government and police officials and peasants who have found the cultivation of coca an economic salvation in difficult times.[3]

Bolivia is also one of the poorest nations in the Western Hemisphere, with a per capita income of $470.[4] In addition, Bolivia has the highest infant mortality rate at 142 deaths per 1000 births and the lowest life expectancy at birth of 50.7 years.[5] Only Haiti has an overall lower level of poverty in the Western Hemisphere. Considering the poverty of the nation, why did Bolivia emerge as a key component of the multibillion dollar narcotics trade?

There are four major reasons for the development of the contemporary Bolivian drug industry. These are: the long-standing weakness of the political center vis-à-vis the periphery; the existence of a traditional coca industry which has cultural significance for the Indian part of the population; developments in the local economy that followed the 1952 revolution; and increased international demand for cocaine. These factors converged in the 1970s during the dictatorship of General Hugo Banzer and were greatly reinforced by the rise and fall of the "cocaine generals" that came to power in General Garciá Meza's 1981 coup. An additional impetus to the expansion of the drug trade in Bolivia was the dire straits that the legal economy found itself in the mid and late 1980s. This was related to the collapse of the London Metals Exchange, which traded tin, and the downturn in oil and natural gas prices in 1986. As tin and natural gas were the nation's major exports, the negative trends in the market had a tremendous impact.

Bolivia has traditionally lacked a high degree of political stability and has had close to 200 coups in its history since its independence from Spain in 1821. One of the major reasons for the lack of political stability has been the inability of the political center to impose its authority on the periphery. Though this trend has been compounded by Argentine and Brazilian involvement (due to interference), the fundamental problem has been strong regionalism aided by poor national communications which are hindered by difficult geographical terrain. Central authority, narrowly concentrated in the capital of La Paz has lacked the population and military strength over time to gain control over the nation's regional patrons. Consequently, La Paz became an arena for regional competitors who fell in coup after coup, with only a few and usually brief democratic interludes.

Bolivia was shaken in 1952 by a radical revolution in which the miners and other labor unions, together with the peasantry and elements of the urban middle class defeated the armed forces. Though the revolution was gradually moderated and the left shunted aside, the impact of the political upheaval on central authority vis-à-vis the periphery was devastating. James A. Malloy noted: "Very quickly after 1952, Bolivia degenerated into a collection of semisovereign fragments only tenuously tied to the national governmental center."[6] Politics throughout the rest of the 1950s remained fluid and regional strongmen or elites were able to consolidate their positions. This is not to argue that the national government totally disappeared: to the contrary, the Bolivian government did implement a number of economic reforms with important consequences for the cocaine industry.

The post–1952 Bolivian governments moved from being revolutionary to reformist and, as they did, there was some concern with reshaping the economy to put the trade and current account balances into favorable terms for the country. The United States, concerned by the 1952 revolution and sensitive to the Bolivian left's flirtations with the Soviet Union, was willing to use its economic assistance as a carrot to moderate the revolution. This was evident in United States aid for road-building and agroindustrial and land-clearing projects.[7] The two areas to benefit from United States aid and the Bolivian government's reforms were Santa Cruz and, to a lesser extent, Beni. As E. Boyd Wennergren and Morris D. Whitaker commented: "Of the relatively small government investment in agriculture, most have gone to the Santa Cruz area in the form of roads, credit price support programs, colonization projects, and the promotion of mechanized modern agriculture."[8] With investment in Santa Cruz's economic development, domestic consumption needs for sugar and rice were soon met, especially as mills were constructed for the processing of both commodities. Cotton and soybeans for export were also cultivated. By 1963, Santa Cruz's economy was booming with its sugar, rice, and cotton industries helping the trade balance.

Although Santa Cruz received governmental and United States assistance, it was not the only region. The ranchers of Beni also benefited from improved roads and communications with the outside world as they soon became one of the major centers of Bolivian beef exporting.

The rural modernization programs undertaken by the Bolivian governments in the late 1950s and early 1960s did not entirely have the results envisioned by the original reform-minded officials that implemented them. The ultimate beneficiaries of rural reform were not the *campesinos*, but in a number of cases, the landlords and merchants. In the two regions discussed, the eastern Department of Beni and Santa Cruz, the rural elite benefited. In the former, this group consisted of ranchers and merchants. The merchants were primarily those involved in the export of cattle, rubber, and Brazil nuts. In the Santa Cruz region, an agrobusiness elite was highly involved in the production and export of sugar, cotton, soybeans, and cattle. They also controlled the sugar and rice mills. This rural elite existed before the rural modernization programs, but benefited by the improved communication system and overall infrastructure. Because of these improvements, they were in a vantage point when the demand for Bolivian cocaine increased in the

1960s. Kevin Healy noted: "The logic of export-oriented agricultural growth of Santa Cruz was the pursuit of quick profits by shifting to the most lucrative crop or processing activity in response to international price changes."[9] In addition, the Santa Cruz-Beni drug barons had certain advantages: large ranches or tracts of land that provided a degree of privacy for the landing of aircraft and because of their relative economic power, they had considerable political clout with local government officials. By the 1980s, the rural elite had made a substantial fortune and expanded its activities into banks, automobile dealerships, and money-exchange and import houses.

The third major group linked to the drug trade after the Santa Cruz and Beni groups, were in the armed forces. The military group, formed from high-ranking officers in the army and air force had linkages to both regional groups and to the various families that dominated the regional industry. In the aftermath of the 1952 revolution, the armed forces were in poor shape: they had been defeated in the revolution, lacked modern equipment, had little training and were divided along personal and regional lines. It was the United States' desire to create a unified and professional armed forces capable of mounting counterinsurgency campaigns and supportive of democracy, that developed a new Bolivian military institution. Indeed, the new armed forces were able to crush local leftist forces and eliminated Ernesto "Che" Guevara's Cuban-supported and officered venture in 1967. At the same time, some of its officers developed an appetite for power and wealth, which led them into coups and, ultimately, into the cocaine industry.

These three groups, the Santa Cruz, Beni, and armed forces "cocaine generals," did not develop apart from each other. There was considerable overlap in their genesis. During the authoritarian regime of General Hugo Banzer Suarez (1971–78), the three groups grew even closer. Banzer's regime was one of the longest in post–1952 Bolivia and was based upon the renovated military, landlords, and *narcotraficantes*. Dunkerley wrote: "Banzer's ability to uphold this system of rigid control was due principally to the unequivocal support he enjoyed for several years from Washington, from an economically expanding and politically ambitious Brazil, and from the dominant agroindustrial interests of Santa Cruz, now the dynamo of the economy as a result of a massive increase in the price of oil and the boom in export agriculture."[10] The reinforcement of this type of regime also came from the advent of similar governments in surrounding countries, such as Argentina, Chile, and Uruguay.

During the Banzerato, the illicit narcotics trade continued to expand. Higher oil, natural gas, and sugar prices, however, blunted rapid expansion as the legal economy was booming. Simply stated, the legal economy provided enough income without developing a heavy trade in coca and coca paste. Tin's contribution to exports rose from $106 million in 1971 to $395.6 million in 1979, while natural gas exports continuously rose from $9.9 million in 1972 to $105 million in 1979.[11] Though the current account balance of payments was in deficit throughout most of the period, the merchandise balance of trade was in surplus.

René Bascopé examined these economic trends and concluded that real expansion of Bolivia's cocaine industry began with the collapse in cotton in 1975–76 and was due to a number of studies sponsored by the Banzer government in close association with the overfinanced members of the *Asociacion de Productores de Algodon* (ADEPA), centered in Santa Cruz.[12] Many in that region had invested in cotton when prices had been good at the beginning of the decade; when prices fell on international markets, increased coca production, with its sale on the contraband market became attractive. These developments, however, need to be clarified: it is likely that expansion commenced in stages, beginning in the 1960s, gaining momentum in the 1970s and flourishing in the1980s. The significant factor is that the legal economy overshadowed the illegal throughout most of the 1970s. In the 1980s, that situation changed with the tin market crash and fall in energy prices. As for direct linkages between the Banzer administration and the *narcotraficantes*, Dunkerley offers the most likely assessment: "there is as yet no firm evidence to prove a concrete policy of unqualified state backing and patronage under Banzer rather than a generally benevolent attitude, occasional assistance and direct involvement on the part of certain individuals."[13]

## THE COCAINE COUP

Bolivia's role in the Latin American drug trade increased greatly in the 1980s, especially after the infamous "cocaine coup" of July 17, 1980. In the aftermath of Banzer's downfall in 1978, the country drifted: two general elections were held, five presidents held office and four coups, one a failure and three successful, were conducted. During one of the civilian administrations a brief antinarcotics campaign was carried out by police chief Jorge Selum. This was not appreciated by Bolivia's *narcotraficantes*, who were also wary of ongoing United States pressure to curtail the drug trade.

Bolivia's leading drug baron in the 1980s was Roberto Suarez Gomez, described by Dunkerley as "head of a traditional *latifundista* family and owner of extensive lands around Santa Ana de Yacuma, far to the north of Beni."[14] Once a cattle farmer, in the 1980s he expanded into coca production, purchased a small fleet of aircraft, and hired a fugitive Nazi, Klaus Barbie, as his security adviser. Barbie organized and headed the "Fiances of Death," Suarez's combination bodyguards/death squads. In a fashion akin to the Colombian *capos*, the Bolivian dealer fostered a

"Robin Hood" image, building and equipping hospitals, paving roads and providing low income housing. He also controlled a tremendous amount of capital, capable of distorting or bailing out the Bolivian economy as he saw fit. Considering Suarez's influence and connections in the government and, more importantly, the armed forces, the drug baron was not likely to brook opposition to his activities. Consequently, Suarez became a leading force in undermining the civilian government of President Gueilier Tejada and preventing the return of Hernan Siles Zuaco to the presidency through elections held in 1980.

Suarez called a meeting of Bolivia's major drug dealers at Club Bavaria in Santa Cruz in the early 1980s.[15] These included Irwin Gasser, Jorge Naller, and Klaus Barbie. With contacts in the armed forces, such as Colonel Luis Arcé Gomez (a relative of Suarez's), the barons were able to contact the army commander in Santa Cruz, General Hugo Echeverra. Through his "good offices" a meeting with General Luis García Meza, the supreme army commander, was arranged for a paltry sum of $800,000. At the meeting with García Meza, the Suarez-led dealers offered the general a bribe of $1,300,000 to lead the coup.[16] There was an additional promise of the vast profits that would be made after the coup in a García Meza-led Bolivia. An additional part of the pact was that Arcé, already involved in drug trading with Colonel Roberto Solomon, was to be given the position of Minister of the Interior which handled antinarcotic affairs.

On July 17, 1980, Bolivia had its 189th coup and García Meza came to power. The involvement of the *narcotraficantes* was well known. As The Economist Intelligence Unit noted: "It remains unfortunately true that the shock troops of the August 1980 coup were not regular military but cocaine financed paramilitary squads. . . ."[17] It was one of the country's more bloody changes of government as the military set out to purge the ranks of its opponents. The head of the socialist party, members of Congress, union leaders and intellectuals were killed, while smaller cocaine dealers had their operations destroyed and their coca bases were seized. Enemies of the state, therefore, were both the political left and smaller nonaligned drug dealers. In addition, Arcé Gomez was promptly made the Minister of Interior, a position that provided him with easy access to all past and ongoing antinarcotic operations. This meant that all United States antinarcotic efforts virtually ended overnight. The cocaine coup was successful in bringing the *narcotraficantes* into an almost dominating position in Bolivia. However, it also set the stage for an eventual confrontation between the cocaine generals and their civilian partners in crime.

There is a strong possibility that the cocaine coup had an "Argentine Connection." Brian Barger, a freelance reporter, identified the 601 Battalion of the Argentine military as being involved in the coup and staying in Bolivia for close to six months after, helping the new junta consolidate its position. What was the Argentine motive? The reporter stated: "Congressional investigators have dug up evidence that the Argentines engineered the 1980 Bolivian coup specifically to benefit from the lucrative cocaine enterprise. As one of them told me,'After the coup, all the 601 Battalion activities were financed with Bolivian cocaine money.' "[18]

The Carter administration was infuriated by the coup. The brutal rise of the cocaine generals collided with both the United States president's human rights and antinarcotics policies. In response, foreign aid of around $127,000,000 was suspended and United States Ambassador Marvin Weisman was withdrawn. As relations deteriorated further Washington also sent home its drug enforcement agents. Initially, this was of little concern to the cocaine generals who found themselves in command of all the means of making substantial profits. As one analyst involved in the DEA's operations in Washington and La Paz said to Freemantle: "It is impossible to calculate the money they made. Think of a preposterous figure, double it and know damn well that you've made a gross underestimate."[19] In a sense, it was "high times" for the cocaine generals.

## THE COCAINE GENERALS FALL FROM GRACE

The García Meza regime quickly expanded its operations throughout the country's cocaine industry. Though never stated, the cocaine generals probably felt that they had the power to take control of the nation's narcotics industry from the Santa Cruz and Beni civilian groups. Even if that was not the intent, the military became overbearing and arrogant with those who had put them in power. It was initially felt that the suspension of United States aid could be covered by drug money, but the antagonism of major *narcotraficantes*, like Suarez, cut off that source of capital. The drug dealers became alienated from the military because of continued pressure against small coca producers, who, in many respects, were important suppliers of the larger dealers. Those supplies were rerouted forcibly, at times, by the military involved in the trade. When Suarez finally went to García Meza to complain, he was forced to pay a substantial bribe for an easing of the pressure. This, according to Dunkerley, set him against the cocaine generals.[20]

The growing irritation of the drug barons, the lack of management of the economy, and the poor international reputation of the García Meza regime set the stage for the government's collapse. A few cosmetic measures at antinarcotic campaigns, moreover, failed to impress the United States and further aggravated the drug barons. In the meantime, the economy began to feel the impact of lower commodity prices. Real GDP growth in 1981 was a negative $-0.3$ percent, with all major sectors of the economy contracting, the worst being manufacturing ($-6.6$ percent) and construction ($-11.9$ percent).[21] External debt pressures were also mounting. As the economic slide began, the cocaine generals were largely pre-occupied by the pursuit of even greater profits.

The drug barons, manipulating growing public unrest, eventually eased García Meza and his close supporters out of office in a relatively bloodless coup in mid–1981. From that point forward, the country drifted both politically and economically. General replaced general and Siles returned to office as a president in 1982 initially constrained by the inability of civilian central authority to gain the complete support of the armed forces or contain the power and influence of the drug barons. However, the divisions between the civilian and military traffickers eventually provided the government an opportunity to strike at some of those in the armed forces who were involved in the trade. Fifteen high-ranking officers were cashiered and others were retired, such as General Alberto Natusch Busch (often mentioned as a drug dealer). Among those cashiered were General García Meza and Colonel Arcé Gomez. The former was charged with smuggling household durables and illicit dealings in precious stones. It was perhaps deemed that outright charges of drug dealing would carry too many political risks. The Siles government, however, did have the courage to capture and extradite Klaus Barbie to France in February 1983. While this was a blow to the country's narcoterror network, it was hardly a mortal wound. Roberto Suarez, already acquitted in a Santa Cruz court on drug charges, remained free, drug enforcement agents were killed and coca producers launched propaganda campaigns for the development of the market for pharmaceuticals and coca-flavored biscuits and drinks.[22]

The government pressure against military traffickers was welcomed by the civilian groups. One study noted that the civilian coca growers were delighted to be freed from the grip of the military and paramilitary would-be monopolists."[23] In a sense, the Siles government helped shunt aside one group of traffickers, helping another regain the dominant role that it had once played.

## ECONOMIC DISEQUILIBRIUM

The Bolivian economy from 1981 to 1986 underwent one of its worst periods of economic adjustment. The economy spun into disequilibrium, pushing the country into several years of crisis. Between 1981 and 1982, the GDP contracted by more than 9 percent and inflation began its rise from 123.5 percent in 1982 to an amazing 11,750 percent in 1985.[24] Bad weather in 1983 hurt the agricultural sector and falling commodity prices in 1984 and early 1985 crushed the mining and industrial sectors. The Siles government sought to implement austerity and adjustment programs, but labor unrest, congressional opposition, and several coup attempts thrawted those efforts. Finally, in 1985 Siles left office and in new elections Victor Paz Estenssoro was elected.

The Paz government was immediately challenged by a rapidly deteriorating economic situation. Bolivia had begun the twentieth century as a leading exporter of tin. By the mid–1980s that commodity had become a liability as international prices plummeted in October 1985. In that month the London Metals Exchange, where tin was traded, closed due to a vast oversupply. An international tin agreement had created stability in the market for several years, but the pressure of a growing number of producers, ranging from Brazil and China to the Cornish mines in the United Kingdom, eventually overwhelmed what the market could absorb. Consequently, the international tin market went into a tailspin with prices plunging to record lows. For Bolivia, already struggling with a number of economic and political problems, this was a disaster and the prospects of a future in which tin was reduced to a minor export loomed. As the Paz administration sought to deal with the tin collapse in late 1985 and early 1986, prices for natural gas, the country's major export, and oil, another significant export, plummeted as well. These developments were tremendous blows to the government's revenue base and made the situation with external debt even worse.[25] Bolivia, beginning in August 1980, had found its external debt burden of over $3 billion beyond its capacity to serve. By year-end 1985, Bolivia's external debt was $3.7 billion.[26]

Paz's stabilization program, implemented soon after he came into power in 1985, slowed inflation to 276 percent by year-end 1986. Although the disequilibrium slowed, the GDP still contracted by 2.9 percent in 1986 and open unemployment exceeded 20 percent of the work force.[27] Bolivia's economic problems effectively reduced the capacity of the legal economy, especially the mining and industrial sectors, to offer the population a livelihood. Though policies were put in place that indicated that the economy was in the process of being turned in the right direction in 1987, the country's standard of living was hard hit and the attractiveness of the only sector still booming, the coca industry, led many ex-miners and otherwise unemployed Bolivians to seek their fortune in the Beni and Santa Cruz areas. The obvious shift in the work force to the coca-producing regions did not go unnoticed by the Paz administration. However, the pressures of external debt and an economy in adjustment meant that the government lacked the resources to combat this development. Further complications were the probable unreliability of elements of the armed forces and the military strength of the *narco-traficantes*.

By the mid–1980s, a complex matrix of drugs, economic development problems, external debt, and a struggle to return the nation to a democratic political system brought Bolivia to a watershed in its history. To allow the situation of political "decontrol" from the center to continue meant opening the door to the possible total collapse of the legal economy, uncontrolled cocaine exports and probable civil war between the areas effectively held by loyal government forces and those dominated, such as Beni department, by the drug barons. And it would not be certain that loyal government forces would win given the military strength of the *narcotraficantes*, the support they have from peasant groups dependent on coca production for their livelihood, and the ability of the drug dealers to bribe members of the armed forces, police and government officials. Paz, therefore, was forced to look for outside assistance in dealing with the power of the drug lords.

## THE UNITED STATES INTERVENTION

In July 1986, United States military personnel were sent into Bolivia in a joint effort with that nation's government to stop the processing and transportation of cocaine. With 170 solidiers in Bolivia and equipped with machinegun-armed Black Hawk helicopters, the Reagan administration signalled its serious intent to tackle what had become a major domestic and hemispheric problem. While the international press, advocates and dissenters discussed the United States government's judgment, motivations, and the legality of the action, an important point was lost in the shuffle. Whether or not the United States-Bolivian action was a success or not, was largely academic. What was significant was that in Bolivia the *narcotraficantes* had once again begun to challenge the government's pretense that it ruled the nation. As one newspaper noted: "Bolivian officials are increasingly worried about the possibility of a political threat from the traffickers. Thus far the drug lords have financed the campaign of some national and local candidates, and have recently purchased controlling interests in local banks and businesses."[28]

Bolivia's production of coca and exportation of cocaine, moreover, had become an obstacle in acquiring badly needed loans and financial assistance from the United States. For the Paz government, the root of United States intervention in Bolivia was over who ruled the nation— the *narcotraficantes* or the duly-elected government in La Paz. Therefore, on July 14, 1986, the United States sent a small contingent to Bolivia, with an announcement in La Paz, by the United States embassy: "The US helicopters and US personnel have been sent to Bolivia at the request of the Bolivian government to provide transportation support to Bolivian civil authorities."[29]

The United States–Bolivian raids struck at major trafficker ranches in the provinces of Yacuma and Magalena in Beni department. Secretly notified in advance, most of the drug barons had already fled to Panama well before antinarcotic forces arrived.[30] Despite that, a coca ranch in Yacuma province was one of the largest uncovered. It consisted of seven large, camouflaged tents in the woods that housed at least seventy-five workers. The operation ultimately uncovered eighteen processing laboratories, capable of producing up to 33,000 pounds of cocaine per week.[31] Moreover, for a brief period coca prices fell to $15–$20 per 100 pounds. The depressed price, it was hoped, would drive some of the smaller producers out and force them to cultivate other, legal crops.

Despite the United States intervention, the effect on the cocaine trade in Bolivia was only temporary. The *narcotraficantes* remain a significant force in the country in the late 1980s and any government sitting in La Paz will be forced to contend with their power. That ongoing threat also suggests that the possibility of another cocaine coup exists.

## THE STRUCTURE OF PERU'S INDUSTRY

The export of coca and cocaine, estimated at over $600 million annually, has become one of Peru's major exports.[32] In 1987, between 98,000–120,000 metric tons of coca leaves were cultivated. By one account, Peru accounts for 55 percent of the world's cocaine, the major market being the United States.[33] Coca, as in Bolivia, was traditionally cultivated and played an important role in local Indian society. The contemporary industry, however, began in the Amazon region in the late 1960s, but did not fully develop until external demand stimulated growth in the 1970s. The complexity of the drug trade in Peru derives from the fact that coca cultivation is the sole source of revenue in many of the isolated mountainous areas and because it grows so well on the Eastern slopes of the Andean mountains, which form a network of river valleys leading into the Amazon basin. The major region is in the Upper Huallaga river valley, where the hillsides are steep and sandy, wet, and well-drained. The major urban center is Tingo María, infamously referred to as "Snow City."[34] From Tingo María, stretching 150 miles north as far as Juanji, it was estimated in mid–1986 that 100,000 peasant families lived entirely off the income produced from coca plantations that covered around 125,000 acres of hillsides.[35] Moreover, the farmer who cultivated a little over a hectare of leaf could earn the equivalent of several thousand dollars a year.[36]

The fertility of the Upper Huallaga for coca production was best summarized by a Peruvian peasant: "God made this valley for coca. I plant coffee; it gets knee-high and it dies. I plant cacao and it turns yellow. Coca—that's all that grows."[37] The large Indian population, which has been traditionally ignored by the succession of governments in Lima, has been heavily involved in both the legal and illegal cultivation of coca. Beyond the financial side of the equation, as in Bolivia, coca consumption has been a regular part of daily life for centuries having both a functional use as well as a ceremonial role. Without coca, Indian culture in Peru faces the prospects of making a major adjustment and, possibly not for the best. Consequently, that segment of Peruvian society has been the most sensitive to antidrug trade campaigns. The sentiments of many Peruvian peasants were summarized by the following comments.:

You know there's a place called Kuwait where they pump oil from under sand that's not good for anything. What would the people do if somebody made the oil illegal? . . . That's illegal (coca production). The bastards come and tear it out. Where will it all end?[38]

The discontent of both Indian and non-Indian peasant groups with coca eradication campaigns has created a difficult situation for the central government. The Belaunde administration (1980–85) cast a relatively blind eye to the drug trade and it was rumored that members of the armed forces were involved though not on the same scale as in Bolivia. Alan Riding noted: "The outflow of coca paste and base from Peru grew dramatically under Mr. García's predecessor, Fernando Belaunde Terry, from 1980–1985."[39] The United States, however, put considerable pressure on the government to do something. Beginning in 1982, the United States helped finance enforcement, eradication and crop substitution programs. This backfired as the local economy suffered from a decline in earnings. In a number of places, these programs opened the door to the Maoist Sendero Luminoso, who were keen to exploit native discontent.[40]

What eventually evolved in Peru's Amazonian region was the emergence of four separate forces—the *narcotraficantes* of Colombian and Peruvian nationalities, the Shining Path guerrillas, the antinarcotics police and the military. Each group had its objectives, which in some cases overlapped and in other cases, conflicted. The antinarcotics police have sought coca eradication, better control over the border region with Colombia, the arrest of traffickers and the destruction of their facilities. This, however, has alienated a fifth group, the peasants (small growers), who resent the destruction of the major livelihood. Peasant unrest has helped attract the Shining Path guerrillas, who want to overthrow the government in Lima and establish a Maoist state. The military, also operating in the same theater as the other groups, wants to destroy the Shining Path forces and perceives coca eradication as a poor policy that will lose the support of the local population. The police and military, therefore, do not share the same objectives. The final group, the drug dealers, find that it is in their interest to have the guerrillas in the area as they keep the military in command of the situation instead of the antinarcotics police. Consequently, there have been occasions in which heavily armed *narcotraficantes* have attacked military patrols disguised as guerrillas, sometimes leaving behind Maoist propaganda. The fighting between these groups picked up considerably in 1983 as violence increased against antidrug forces in the Upper Huallaga Valley. A series of violent attacks by traffickers (and/or possibly guerrillas) on police units and eradication workers in the region led to the November 1984 torture and murder of nineteen members of a United States-financed coca-eradication team, and subsequently, to the murder of seventeen United States-financed eradicators.[41]

## THE DRUG-INSURGENCY NEXUS

There has been considerable discussion that the Sendero Luminoso and the *narcotraficantes* have joined forces in Peru. Freemantle stated: "There is still another drug-related problem creating difficulties for the government. Peru has a group of revolutionary guerrillas—the 'Sendero Luminoso' (Shining Path)—who have reached an arrangement, similar to that which exists in Colombia, to provide protection for some Peruvian coca plantations in exchange for finance and weapons."[42] He supports his claim by holding up as evidence the assassination in October 1983 by the revolutionaries of General Carlos Herrera, director of the plains-clothes branch of the police training school and the guerrilla offensive in August 1984 that ousted the United States-trained antinarcotics service from the Tingo María area. He also linked the Sendero Luminoso to Cuba, suggesting "backing and guidance."[43]

Rensselaer W. Lee, III concurred with the drug-insurgency nexus theory in Peru. His conviction was formed by both United States government and Latin American sources. One of those sources was President Belaunde, who stated in a 1983 interview with *El Tiempo*:

From where do you think the M–19 Movement obtained so much money? And from where is Sendero Luminoso principally financed? It is clear that they get some funds from bank robberies and kidnappings; yet the fact is that the bulk of their budget comes from narcoterrorists.[44]

Others have disagreed with the perception of a drug-insurgency nexus having developed in Peru. They argue there is no evidence for these assertions, that too little is known of the Sendero Luminoso to speculate, and that such claims are part of a United States-backed disinformation campaign to link the Latin American left to the nefarious drug trade. The reality of the situation is probably somewhere in between: links probably do exist between the Sendero Luminoso and local and Colombian *narcotraficantes*, but the ties to Cuba are not likely. Coletta Youngers of the Washington Office on Latin America felt that the Sendero Luminoso were originally opposed to the drug trade, but later changed their thinking on the matter.[45] Based on conversations with people in Peru in late 1987, she felt that there was a probability that the Sendero Luminoso had allied themselves to the small producers and were seeking to eliminate the Peruvian middlemen and deal directly with the Colombian *narcotraficantes*. This would allow them to negotiate a better price for the small producers, who would then be taxed on the profits. Those taxes would then go into the "war budget." As for usage of cocaine, Sendero Luminoso was rumored to be against it.

The possibility of Peru's *narcotraficantes* and the Sendero Luminoso forming an alliance in parts of the country would mean that the drug-insurgency nexus exists in another Latin American country. In Peru, this combination could form a substantial threat to the official state in Lima. Considering the possibility of that development, the newly elected government of President Alan García made the war on drugs a priority. As Garcia stated at his inaugural address, July 1985: "A historical scourge threatens our country—the drug traffic, whose temptation to quick riches corrodes consciences and destroys institutions. Our country and others cannot be identified internationally as exporters of poison."[46]

The Peruvian situation has been further complicated by other factors. The drug trade has not been the only problem confronting the García administration. First and foremost, the country's external debt of $14 billion was well beyond Peru's capacity to repay. It was initially rumored that some within the government actually contemplated accepting an offer from one of the drug barons to repay the nation's debt in return for an amnesty. The debt crisis was dealt with in another fashion as García soon linked debt repayments with 10 percent of export earnings.

On the political front, García's party, the *Alianza Popular Revolucionaria Americana* (APRA) had historically had poor relations with the armed forces. There were no guarantees that the armed forces would remain in the barracks with an Aprista as president. García's popularity, however, functioned as a buffer against that development. While García established control over the formal political system, the Sendero Luminoso posed a problem in the southern part of the country and a few regions in the north. Their tactics of assassinations and bombings kept much of the country, including the capital of Lima on edge. Considering the wide range of problems confronting the new government, the anti-narcotics campaign was important, but not the uppermost priority.

The García government's economic program of debt repayment reduction and capital infusion into the domestic economy had positive results in 1986, when the growth rate was 8.5 percent. Despite the activity on the economic front, the government's antidrug campaign did achieve some results. Under García, significant quantities of coca paste were seized, laboratories were dismantled, and the air force bombed twelve clandestine airstrips in the northeastern jungle region under the auspices of Operation Condor. In November 1985, García returned control of the Upper Huallaga Valley to civilian authorities who returned to the offensive against the trade. The response to government pressure was the targeting of APRA officials. This was reflected by the assassination of the APRA mayor of Auycayacu in February 1986. Auycayacu is north of Tingo María and, likewise, sits in the heart of Peru's coca production area. Police and municipal officials felt that the guerrillas carried out the murder as "payment" in part to the *narcotraficantes*.[47] If this was indeed the case, it dovetailed nicely with the Sendero Luminoso campaign of destabilization.

In 1986 and 1987 the Peruvian government continued to cooperate with Brazil, Colombia, and Ecuador in antinarcotic campaigns in the "Amazonian Triangle." Considering the difficult terrain, the weaker representation of state authorities in the frontier region, and the ability of *narcotraficantes* to move across borders and bribe poorly paid officials, the drug trade and coca cultivation continued. Alan Garcia's antinarcotics policy has been founded on good intentions, but his domestic economic policies, such as the nationalization of the country's banks, and external policy debt repayment to 10 percent of exports have alienated segments of the middle class and the armed forces. Moreover, the continued existence of the *narcotraficantes*, the Sendero Luminoso, and another urban-based Marxist terrorist group, the Tupac Amaro, leaves parts of the country out of the government's control.

## CONCLUSION

Bolivia and Peru have surpassed Colombia as the major producers of coca. While much of the network throughout the Americas remains dominated by the Colombians, local drug barons with networks of their own have emerged in both countries. Furthermore, the *narcotraficantes* have been, and continue to be, highly linked to terrorist activities, with ties to the far left as well as the far right. There is also growing domestic consumption in these nations.

The many similarities between the two nations is not complete. Central authority in Peru has traditionally been stronger than in Bolivia. While Peru has had its share of political instability, its record has not been as problematic. Bolivia remains one of the few countries in the world, possibly the only one, that could conceivably be taken over by the cocaine mafia. As one North American commercial banker, who had visited Bolivia in November 1987, commented: "I wouldn't be surprised if the cocaine mafia took over—it probably won't take much."[48] Peru has many problems, but the *narcotraficantes* do not present such a formidable threat.

## NOTES

1. John Crabtree, Gavan Duffy and Jenny Pearce, *The Great Tin Crash: Bolivia and the World Tin Market* (London: Latin America Bureau, 1987), p. 83. Also see *The New York Times*, March 2, 1988, p. A7.

2. According to the most recent report by Bolivia's Chamber of Deputies, quoted in *Latin America Regional Reports Andean Group*, April 9, 1987, p. 7.

3. Bolivian government estimate cited in "Bolivia asks, gets US aid vs. drug lords," *The Times of the Americas*, July 23, 1986, p. 1.

4. World Bank, *World Bank Development Report 1987* (New York: Oxford University Press, 1987), p. 202.

5. Inter-American Development Bank, *Economic and Social Progress in Latin America 1987 Report* (Washington, D.C.: Inter-American Development Bank, 1987), p. 235.

6. James A. Malloy, "Revolutionary Politics," in James A. Malloy and Richard S. Thorn (editors), *Beyond the Revolution: Bolivia since 1952* (Pittsburgh: University of Pittsburgh Press, 1971), p. 136.

7. Richard S. Thorn, "The Economic Transformation," in Malloy and Thorn, (editors) *Beyond the Revolution* pp. 188–190; L. Gill, *Commercial Agriculture and Peasant Production: A Study of Agrarian Capitalism in Northern Santa Cruz, Bolivia* (Ph.D. dissertation, Columbia University, 1984); E. Boyd Wennergren and Morris D. Whitaker, *The Status of Bolivian Agriculture* (New York: Praeger Publishers, 1975), pp. 227–230; and S. Eckstein, "El capitalismo mundial y la revolucion agraria en Bolivia," *Revista Mexicana de Sociologia* (1979), XLI, pp. 457–478.

8. E. B. Wennergren and M. D. Whitaker, *The Status of Bolivian Agriculture*, p. 40.

9. Kevin Healy, "The Boom Within the Crisis: Some Recent Effects of Foreign Cocaine Markets on Bolivian Rural Society and Economy," in Deborah Pacini and Christine Franquemont (editors), *Coca and Cocaine: Effects on People and Policy in Latin America* (Petersborough, New Hampshire: Transcript Publishing Company, 1986), p. 105.

10. James Dunkerly, *Rebellion in the Veins: Political Struggle in Bolivia, 1952–1982* (London: Verso Editions, 1984), p. 201.

11. International Monetary Fund, *International Financial Statistics Yearbook 1986* (Washington, D.C.: International Monetary Fund, 1986), p. 229.

12 .René Bascopé, *La Veta Blanca: Coca y cocaina en Bolivia* (La Paz: Edimones Aquí, 1982), p. 90.

13. James Dunkerley, *Rebellion in the Viens*, p. 315.

14. Ibid., p. 316.

15. Brian Freemantle, *The Fix: Inside the World Drug Trade* (New York: Tom Doherty Associates, Inc., 1986), p. 240.

16. Ibid., pp. 240–241.

17. The Economist Intelligence Unit, *Quarterly Economic Review of Peru, Bolivia*, No. 1, 1983, p. 19.

18. Brain Barger, "The Contras and Cocaine," *Penthouse*, December 1987, p. 168.

19. Freemantle, *The Fix*, p. 242.

20. Dunkerley, *Rebellion in the Veins,* p. 321.

21. Inter-American Development Bank, *Economic and Social Progress in Latin America 1986 Report* (Washington, D.C.: Inter-American Development Bank, 1986), p. 212.

22. Economist Intelligence Unit, *Quarterly Economic Review of Peru, Bolivia,* No. 2, 1983, p. 24.

23. Ibid., p. 23.

24. Inter-American Development Bank, *Economic and Social Progress in Latin America 1987 Report,* p. 238.

25. Ibid., p. 239.

26. Organization for Economic Cooperation and Development, *External Debt Statistics: The Debt and Other External Liabilities of Developing, CMEA and Certain Other Countries and Territories* (Paris: Organization for Economic Cooperation and Development, 1987), p. 16.

27. Inter-American Development Bank, *Economic and Social Progress in Latin American 1987 Report,* p. 238.

28. "Bolivia asks, gets, U.S. aid vs. drug lords," *The Times of the Americas,* July 23, 1986, p. 1.

29. Ibid.

30. "U.S.-supported drug raids bring mixed results in Bolivia," *The Times of the Americas,* August 6, 1986, p. 1.

31. "Bolivians continue drug raids, US troops leave," *The Times of the Americas,* November 26, 1986, p. 1.

32. Jane Monahan, "Peru," in *The Latin America and Caribbean Review 1987* (Harmondsworth, United Kingdom: World of Information, 1987), p. 121.

33. Alan Riding, "Peru's Forces Press Ahead in Drug War," *The New York Times,* August 17, 1986, p. A12.

34. Freemantle, *The Fix,* p. 250.

35. Alan Riding, "Peru's Forces."

36. David L. Strug, "The Foreign Politics of Cocaine: Comments on a Plan to Eradicate the Coca Leaf in Peru," in Pacini and Franquemont, *Coca and Cocaine,* p. 78.

37. Quoted from William Montalbano, "Coca Valley: Peru Jungle Surrealism," *The Los Angeles Times,* December 2, 1985; *Information Service Latin America,* December 1985, p. 315.

38. William Montalbano, ibid., p. 315.

39. Alan Riding, "Peru's Forces," etc. Also suggested in Strug, "The Foreign Politics of Cocaine," p. 78.

40. Riordan Roett, "Peru: The Message from Garcia," *Foreign Affairs,* 61, 2 (1985), p. 251.

41. President's Commission on Organized Crime, *America's Habit: Drug Abuse, Drug Trafficking, and Organized Crime* (Washington, D.C.: U.S. Government Printing Office, March 1987), pp. 169–170.

42. Brian Freemantle, *The Fix,* p. 254.

43. Quoted in Rensselar W. Lee III, "The Latin American Drug Connection," *Foreign Policy* 61 (Winter 1985–86), p. 155.

44. William Montalbano, "Coca Valley," p. 310.

45. Personal communication with Coletta Youngers of the Washington Office on Latin America in Washington, D.C., held on January 5, 1988.

46. Inter-American Development Bank, *Economic and Social Progress in Latin America 1987 Report*, p. 376.

47. "Peruvian mayor shot dead by guerrillas," *The Financial Times*, February 27, 1986, p. 3.

48. Private conversation with a commercial banker in Washington, D.C., in November 1987.

# 5

# All Things to All People: Mexico

## INTRODUCTION

Mexico and the United States are bound together by history, trade, movement of people, and the debt crisis. The United States is Mexico's major trade partner, it is the destination of the vast majority of its migrants, and North American banks are the primary holders of Mexico's external debt. Conversely, Mexico is the United States' third largest trade partner, an important source of imported oil, and a highly popular destination for tourists and retirees. Mexico is also one of the major sources in the United States market for heroin, marijuana and, most recently, cocaine smuggled through the country from South America. The expansion of Mexico's role in the Latin American drug trade in the 1980s greatly strained relations between the two nations, raising serious questions about sovereignty, intervention, and the limits of interdependence. Accusations about official corruption in Mexico and charges by leading United States politicians that the Latin country was not doing its "fair share" in the war on drugs made the issue all the more bitter.

It is the purpose of this chapter to examine Mexico's role in the Latin American drug trade. Although Mexico does not play the same pivotal role as Colombia nor is it a major source of cocaine like Bolivia and Peru, it remains highly significant to the United States market due to geographical proximity and the porous nature of the border. Mexico's drug industry has three components: the production and export of herion and marijuana and the transshipment of cocaine from Bolivia, Colombia, and Peru to the United States. As in Bolivia, Colombia, and Peru the drug trade has become a local problem in terms of addiction, corruption and part of an overall concern about where the country is heading. Contrary to certain views in the United States that Mexicans do not care about the drug trade, there was a growing awareness and concern in the mid–1980s, but the perceived pushiness of the northern country has led to sometimes unforeseen outcomes south of the border.

## BACKGROUND TO THE TRADE

The state of events between Mexico and the United States in terms of the drug issue in the late 1980s cannot be understood without some background knowledge of the evolution of the trade in Mexico. Heroin first became big business in the United States in the 1920s and Mexico was not in the picture. The trade was first dominated by New York City's Jewish community, but by the late 1930s the *La Cosa Nostra* became involved, having a network that extended from France, Asia, and the Middle East. World War II, however, interrupted these linkages causing heroin traders to look elsewhere. With its lightly guarded 1,700-mile border with the United States and extensive regions suitable for both opium poppy cultivation and refining, nearby Mexico became attractive. By the late 1940s, Mexico's heroin industry was well-established.

Mexico's narcotic business in the 1960s was largely based on heroin and marijuana, although some cocaine was smuggled through the country from South America. While heroin was produced domestically, a large percentage came from France. The development of the heroin business in Europe and the Middle East in the 1960s was controlled by the "French Connection." This operation used Turkish morphine base that was refined in Marseilles, France. The finished product was then shipped to Sicily or Montreal and then into the United States. Mexico was also part of the French Connection. In 1969 about 80 percent of the heroin smuggled into the United States was said to be the French variety.[1] French heroin was brought into Mexico by ship at Vera Cruz and by plane to Mexico City. From those locations it headed north in trucks or small planes.

Mexico's marijuana production underwent a boom period in the 1960s. Produced mainly in the northern Sierra Madre mountains, thousands of small farmers were involved in what became a lucrative enterprise. Simply stated, the peasants involved could make considerably more money growing marijuana than they could any other cash crop. Growing marijuana in remote mountainous areas, the farmer would harvest and bring it into town on pack donkeys. In the small towns, themselves somewhat isolated, dealers made their purchases, usually at $4 per kilo (2.2 pounds).[2] The dealers, some with links to the big family organizations, had ready cash, small warehouses and contacts with the local police. They would take the marijuana, moisten the grey-green leaves and flowers with sugarwater, pack and re-dry them in one kilo blocks, wrap them in cellophane or newspaper and accumulate enough to prepare a truckload for shipment. In 1969, each kilo that reached Los Angeles was worth $75 and moving northwards the value increased with it reaching a price of $150 in Minneapolis. In addition, Mexican *narcotraficantes* reduced marijuana into the more potent hashish, which sold for $500 to $650 per kilo.

The flow of these drugs, together with barbiturates, amphetamines, LSD, and other hallucinogens, went northwards along Highway 15 and into the United States. The United States' reaction to this was epitomized by a report to President Nixon that concluded: "Only a massive, continuous effort, directed by the highest officials in Mexico, will significantly curtail the production and refinement of marijuana and other dangerous drugs."[3] On the Mexican side, there were efforts to fight the drug trade, but it was hardly regarded as a pressing issue. Furthermore, Mexico lacked the adequate resources to contend with the increasing volume of the trade. In 1969, Mexico's Federal Judicial police, who had jurisdiction over narcotics violations, numbered only 264 agents and few aircraft for observation, and facilities for crop eradication were lacking.[4]

A growing usage of drugs in the United States and frustration with the seeming inability of the Mexican government to act, eventually led to the Nixon administration's launching of Operation Intercept in early September 1969. Some 2,000 customs and patrol agents were posted along the border in what was announced by the North American officials as "the largest peace-time search and seizure operation by civil authorities."[5] Tijuana was declared "off limits" to United States military personnel and it was hinted that other border towns, including Juarez and Nogales, might also be declared off limits unless the Mexican government acted more effectively in combating the drug trade. Such actions were intended as a slap on the wrist as these towns depended on the tourist trade from the United States for a substantial portion of their revenues.

Though the drug trade on land was temporarily reduced, the results of the "border blockade" were less than spectacular; not a single major shipment of heroin or marijuana was intercepted. At the same time, Operation Intercept became a major source of tension between the United States and Mexico. This was because the latter government was angered at being given no prior warning, which implied that it could not be trusted with a secret.[6] Consequently, the operation was perceived as an affront to Mexico's national honor. Moreover, the blockade along the border, that paralyzed traffic for several days, threatened across-the-border trade and commerce. Merchants in the United States also found the situation detrimental to their businesses and were vocal in complaining.

An unexpected development was that Mexico's vocal discontent jeopardized the Nixon administration's desire to have better relations with Latin America. This was soon apparent when President Gustavo Díaz Ordaz joked in early October 1969 that the name of the International Friendship Dam inaugurated on the Río Grande a month earlier by himself and Nixon should be changed to Dam Friendship.[7] The Mexican president later noted that Operation Intercept had raised a "wall of suspicion" in relations between the United States and his country. The Nixon administration's unilateral movement was perceived as a lack of "good neighbor" attitude toward Latin America in general.

The United States finally relented and eased pressure along the border. An agreement was concluded between the two governments with the United States providing Mexico with $1,000,000 to eliminate plantations for both opium poppies and marijuana. Operations were then carried out in the rugged Sierra Madre mountain states of Durango, Sinaloa, and Chihuahua. One immediate result was the Mexican army's seizure of a 250-acre marijuana farm in the southern State of Oaxaca. This indicated that the transition had been made from Operation Intercept to the newly proclaimed "Operation Cooperation."

The Mexican drug business received another boost when the French Connection collapsed in 1972. This was because the Turkish government, under considerable pressure from the United States, banned opium production. Consequently, the global industry changed: Amsterdam replaced Marseilles as the European drug capital and in the United States distribution centers expanded beyond New York to Chicago, Los Angeles, and Miami. At the same time, Mexico replaced Turkey as one of the major sources of heroin in the United States. Within five years, Mexico was the leading source.

Mexico's percentage of the United States market for heroin and marijuana expanded considerably in the late 1970s. Some estimates put the share of United States imports of both drugs at over 80 percent.[8] This situation resulted in renewed efforts of cooperation, such as Operation Condor, in which the Mexican government pushed crop eradication and better enforcement. The combined pressure on both sides of the border was temporarily effective and by the early 1980s the narcotics issue was secondary. As Lowenthal noted: "Periodic Mexican arrests of U.S. citizens in Mexico for illegal possession of or commerce in drugs became more of an issue than the flow of narcotics into this country."[9]

## MEXICO'S DRUG TRADE AND THE ECONOMIC CRISIS

There is an indirect, yet important relationship between Mexico's debt crisis and the expansion of the drug trade during the 1980s. A brief background about Mexico's economic development is, therefore, required as it provides certain insights as to why the trade "took off" in the 1980s and why attempts to curb it have been largely ineffectual.

In the 1960s and 1970s, the "Mexican miracle" occurred as the Latin American nation developed its manufacturing sector behind protectionist walls. Higher energy prices also helped the country financially throughout the late 1970s, especially after the discovery of massive new reserves in 1977. The Mexican economy enjoyed a period of strong expansion in the late 1970s and early 1980s based on the exploitation of oil and natural gas resources. Management of the economy, most of which was under state control, lacked vision and was weakened by high levels of corruption. Moreover, the government's rapid expansion into the economy in the late 1970s and early 1980s was accomplished at the cost of extensive foreign borrowing. Mexico's external debt expanded from $11.5 billion in 1975 to $91.5 billion in 1982. By 1982, debt repayment was beyond Mexico's ability and the nation was forced to reschedule in August over what became known as the "Mexican weekend."[10]

In 1983–84 the de la Madrid administration (in office in 1982) adopted an International Monetary Fund-supervised program, which halved inflation, cut imports and the public sector deficit by two-thirds, produced bumper trade and current account surpluses and rebuilt reserves. However, the government subsequently allowed the economy to overheat badly in the run up to the July 1985 mid term congressional and gubernatorial elections. As domestic demand recovered, inflation revived, the peso, trade and current account surpluses sank, and non-oil exports fell. Though the ruling *Partido Revolucionarío Institucional* (PRI) won the elections, as most analysts knew it would through fraud and actual support, the price was a growing economic crisis that was considerably worsened by the damages caused by two earthquakes in 1985 and the fall in oil prices in late 1985 and 1986. Consequently, the economy contracted by 3.5 percent in 1986, inflation rose from 58 percent to 106 percent, the current account shifted from a small surplus in 1985 to a $2 billion deficit and international reserves fell from $5.6 billion to $4.8 billion.[11] Moreover, Mexico was forced to reschedule its external debt for the second time, which was a protracted, but ultimately successful exercise.

The ups and downs of Mexico's economy had a profound impact on the country's social and political structure. Per capita income fell from $2,646 in 1980 to $1,598 in 1986.[12] Many social programs were shelved and others had their budgets cut substantially. Wages also suffered. The severity of this situation prompted the Secretary of Finance and Public Credit, Gustavo Petricioli, to comment in July 1987: "The persistent fall in our income and the scarcity of outside financing made it impossible for us to continue absorbing all the effects of the crisis at the domestic level. It would have meant a high social cost in terms of production, employment and public welfare."[13]

It is highly probable that the difficult position of the Mexican economy in the 1980s was a major impetus for the drug trade. Once again, austerity measures, low salaries, rising unemployment, and a certain degree of alienation from the formal political system made the big profits of the drug trade appealing. This appeal was not limited to one class of Mexicans, but penetrated all levels of society as it had in Bolivia, Colombia, and Peru.

While the economy underwent a severe crisis, the nation's ruling party also suffered a crisis of identity. The PRI since the revolution in the early part of the twentieth century had dominated Mexico by a policy of inclusiveness based on co-optation and coercion as well as outright popular support. Indeed, the PRI presided over a considerable span of stable government, especially when compared to many other developing countries in Latin America and elsewhere. The economic crisis in the 1980s, however, hampered the party's ability to "buy" support as it had in the past by implementing popular programs that usually met a social demand. Confronted by a more vocal opposition, especially in the country's northern states, the PRI found itself in the late 1980s challenged both politically and economically. The situation was further complicated by an internal party debate about the need to "democratize" the party and the political system.[14] Into this complex matrix of issues and challenges, the drug trade was not at the forefront. While it was important and did receive some attention, the country's economic crisis dominated. Only when the drug issue was pushed from the outside was narcotics briefly pushed to the front.

## THE NEXT WAVE: THE MID AND LATE 1980S

The surge in heroin and marijuana exports into the United States in the 1970s was followed by a decline at the very end of the decade and into the first years of the next decade. This is not to imply that the drug trade evaporated or totally disappeared in the early 1980s. The drug trade continued, but enforcement and eradication measures reduced the inflow and other nations, like Colombia, were competitive for the same products. However, by the mid–1980s, narcotics exports were on the increase. As one Mexican journalist commented: "The law of supply and demand teaches us that where there is a market, there will always be someone to supply it."[15] In the mid–1980s demand increased and Mexican *narcotraficantes*, in a strategic position, were able to respond.

Mexico, as already mentioned, had a lightly guarded and porous border and the existence of extensive regions that were well-suited for undetected cultivation and refining of heroin and marijuana. To these "traditional" comparative advantages, Mexico's *narcotraficantes* benefited from stricter eradication programs in Colombia and Peru, the preoccupation of Mexico's government with the dire economic conditions caused by the debt crisis, corruption within the country's law enforcement system, and a substantial upswing in drug demand in the United States.[16] The combination of these factors brought in the new wave of drugs from Mexico into the United States.

The dominant force in Mexico's drug trade for almost three decades has been the Herrera family which is based in the state of Durango in the Sierra Madre area. With a family network that extended to Chicago and Joliet, Illinois, the Herrera family claimed between 3,000–5,000 members, included naturalized United States citizens and illegal aliens. As one United States government study commented: "Since the early 1970s the Jaime Herrera Navarres organization has been a major heroin smuggling power operative between Mexico and the United States.[17] Despite Jaime Herrera's 1978 conviction and imprisonment, the organization continued operations. This was evident in July 1985 when 135 persons in the United States, consisting of eight different Herrera-related distribution rings, were indicted in Chicago in drug trafficking charges. Heroin and marijuana were smuggled into the United States at El Paso, Texas. From that point, it was moved to Chicago for distribution across the nation. According to the same United States government report, the gross annual profits of these groups, that were only a small fragment of the entire family empire, stood at $200 million.[18]

In the late 1980s, an increasing amount of heroin was produced in Mexico and at least 40 percent of marijuana used in the United States in 1985 and 1986 was produced in Mexico.[19] Traffickers from South America also "rediscovered" Mexico as a convenient transshipment point for cocaine. Transportation of these items ranged from people crossing the frontier on foot to trucks, mules, and aircraft. One commentator noted: "Mexican marijuana is smuggled across the United States border in amounts ranging from a few pounds up to several tonnes, depending on the mode of transportation. According to United States drug officials, traffickers use people on foot, cars, campers, and trucks to transport the drug across the border."[20]

Drug smuggling into the United States from Mexico also had its gruesome side. While the more traditional ways have included packets of cocaine in shaving cream cans, tooth paste tubes, lotion jars, perfume bottles, and shoe heels, other methods involved the swallowing of capsules. These capsules are made from surgical gloves, which have the rubber fingers cut of, filled with cocaine and sealed. Unless the stomach is based with bananas and oil, there is a danger that the stomach's digestive acids will eat through the plastic. In 1984, a woman smuggler died in Mexico City when one of the capsules had opened in her digestive system and pure cocaine had leaked.[21] A more hideous case occurred when a couple at Mexico City airport were caught seeking to smuggle cocaine into the country. They had kidnapped a baby, killed it, split him open along the back and stuffed him with several kilos of cocaine.[22].

Many of the organizations, like the Herrera family, are horizontally and vertically involved, controlling production, transportation, smuggling, enforcement, and marketing to distribution areas. The only area not touched are street sales which are left to native dealers. In many respects the business of producing marijuana had not changed since the 1960s, except perhaps in the area of refining and transporting the merchandise. There have also been cases of marijuana plantations in remote areas of the country where local peasants have been forced to work in slavelike conditions.

Mexico has its own drug consumption problem, though it is not usually brought out into the open nor is it as significant as that in Colombia or the United States. Drug use largely consists of marijuana smoking, inhalable chemicals and a few man-made drugs. Heroin and cocaine consumption have not been substantial. In a *Mexico Today* interview in May 1985, then Attorney General Dr. Sergio Garcia Ramirez commented that his country was conducting an antidrug campaign as "a battle for the health of Mexico but perhaps even more for the health of other nations."[23] He further asserted that Mexico did not have the problem with drugs being grown in the country for domestic consumption as some countries did, and that there was hardly any use of heroin and cocaine.

One reason advanced for Mexico's lack of a serious consumption of cocaine and heroin was advanced by Fernando Lara Pastrana, the head of the toxic laboratory in Toluca, a city 42 miles northeast of Mexico City. Pastrana felt that "we are too poor a country to actually consume drugs like cocaine and heroin."[24] A number of studies conducted in Mexico concluded that alcohol was the country's most harmful addiction, followed by marijuana.[25] Simply stated there was greater usage of alcohol (in part because it was legal) and marijuana (which remains illegal) due to easy access and relative cheapness.

Mexico's illegal drug industry in the late 1980s was much more resilient than it was in decades past and is heavily oriented to exports, not domestic consumption. As in Bolivia and Colombia, the Mexican *narcotraficantes* have become part of the landscape and owned segments of the legal economy. Mexico's drug trade was probably worth at least $1–2 billion annually in terms of sales and possibly $300–350 million in capital inflow into Mexico. Considering the difficult economic situation the country has been in since 1982, the *narcotraficantes* play a role in the national economy that cannot be overlooked.

## MEXICAN-UNITED STATES RELATIONS

The pivotal year in Mexican-United States drug relations was 1985. North American irritation with the Mexican government's seeming inability to control *narcotraficantes* and perceived official corruption became front and center in what evolved into a tense situation. Renewed United States efforts at interdiction off the Florida coast led Colombian drug producers to forge a new alliance with Mexican crime families to ship cocaine through Mexico despite the route being longer and more costly.[26] It was speculated by the DEA that cocaine was transported through Mexico by Colombians who paid Mexican accomplices around 10 percent of each shipment in return for storage and protection.

The narcotics issue became explosive on February 7, 1985 with the murder of DEA agent Enrique Camerena Salazar and his Mexican pilot, Alfredo Zavala Avelar. The former was kidnapped by four gunmen as he left the United States consulate in Guadalajara. Inquiries about the matter with Mexican police were less than satisfactory: Freemantle claimed that the police were, in fact, bribed to do nothing.[27] The situation changed, however, when DEA chief Francis "Bud" Mullen, flew to Mexico and demanded action.[28] This was followed by Attorney General French Smith sending a sharply worded telegram to his Mexican counterpart and President Reagan sent a personal letter to de la Madrid requesting assistance in the matter.

The incident became even more ugly when Camerena's and Zavala's tortured bodies were found on March 6, 1985 at a remote ranch 60 miles southwest of Guadalajara. Acting on a tip, Mexican police went to the ranch, where they became involved in a firefight with traffickers that left five *narcotraficantes* and one policeman dead. One of the men thought responsible was a well-known trafficker, Rafael Caro Quintero, who was intercepted two days later by Mexican federal and state police alerted by the DEA. Quintero, however, was able to bribe his way free, escaping to Costa Rica. The Mexican Federal Judicial Police commander involved in the incident, Armando Pavón Reyes, later admitted that he accepted a $275,000 bribe to allow Caro Quintero's plane to leave Guadalajara airport.[29] Pavón was sentenced to a jail term in Mexico City for this. After serving a short period he managed to bribe his way to freedom.

Caro Quintero was not long at large. In April 1985, he was captured along with four heavily armed bodyguards in Costa Rica by local authorities acting on a DEA tip. Found with the *narcotraficante* was the kidnapped, 17-year-old daughter of a wealthy Mexican businessman and brother of an official in the PRI. It appears that Mexico's *narcotraficantes* followed many of the methods of their counterparts in South America. Despite Caro Quintero's precautions, he was sent back to Mexico where he was put on trial and sentenced to prison.

The ripples from the Camarena murder did not stop with Quintero. Ernesto Fonseca, a major trafficker sought in the case, was arrested soon thereafter with twenty-three other people (many of them federal enforcement agents).[30] Fonseca admitted to trafficking, paying bribes, and his involvement in planning Camerena's kidnapping. However, he denied murdering the DEA agent, accusing still another trafficker, Miguel Felíx Gallardo of that act. Felíx Gallardo, however, continued to live a somewhat open and flamboyant life-style in Mexico. According to James Mills, a source in the Mexican attorney general's office commented that Felíx Gallardo "is a trafficker of such magnitude and wealth that he was able to bribe so many influential officials in high government positions, including the attorney general's office and the MFJP (Mexican Federal Judicial Police) that if it were to reveal the identities of these individuals it would create too much chaos and havoc in the government of Mexico."[31] It was alleged that after the DEA agent's death, Gallardo was the house guest of Antonio Toledo Corro, the governor of the State of Sinaloa.[32] There were also rumors that Gallardo stayed with another, unnamed governor as well. Though Toledo denied these charges, United States frustration with the slowness of the Mexican investigation into Camerena's murder, left this a sore point. On the Mexican side, there was considerable embarrassment, especially at a time when the PRI was under attack at home for many of the same reasons (corruption and fraud). It is possible that the PRI refused to move against these governors as it would cause further embarrassment. Moreover, the Mexican authorities wanted hard evidence from the United States agencies; something that the North Americans were averse to doing considering the lack of protection Mexican authorities could offer. It was also felt that if the information was provided, United States informants would be compromised. The matter of tackling PRI governors, therefore, was not pursued, but was left to fester as a growing United States well of frustration.

The drug issue was hardly allowed to fade from the front of Mexican-United States issues when a United States Customs Service patrol officer, Glenn Miles, was killed by traffickers in April 1986 on the United States side of the border.[33] Miles' death helped raise the temperature of relations between the two nations, but it was the Helms hearings in June 1986 that brought mutual recriminations.

In the United States, considerable pressure had built concerning Mexico's role in the drug trade. In a United States government report released earlier in 1986, it was noted that Mexico's efforts at drug eradication were the "principal disappointment" of 1985.[34] The report by the State Department's Bureau of International Narcotics Matters also stated: "The indication at year's end was that Mexico was perhaps once again the leading exporter of marijuana to the United States, and the single largest of heroin."[35] Further discontent came from Camerena's murder and the expectation that Mexico was to produce between twenty-one and forty-five metric tons of opium in 1986 and around 3,000 tons of marijuana.[36]

United States frustration and indignation about the seeming inability of the Mexican government to come to terms with the drug trade erupted in June 1986 during President de la Madrid's visit to Washington, D.C. The eruption did not come from the White House, but from a subcommittee of the Senate Foreign Relations Committee presided over by Republican Senator Jesse Helms. There had been earlier accusations about corruption in Mexico, including claims that both former presidents Luis Echeverria (1970–76) and Jose Lopez Portillo (1976–82) were involved in billion dollar corruption schemes, while the former police chief of Mexico City, a crony of the later president was reputed to be heavily involved in the drug trade. The Helms hearings were to be more sensational. During the hearings, Mexico was taken to task for its official corruption, the drug trade, immigration and the questionability of its claims to be a democratic nation. Helms' testiness did little to calm the situation. He accused Mexican officials of fraud, corruption, and links to drug trafficking. The Mexicans were quick to point out that their army devoted a quarter of its total manpower to antidrug activities. Furthermore, the Mexican Ambassador to the United Nations issued a statement saying that his country allocated 40 percent of the budget of its Attorney General's office to combating narcotics and pointedly suggested that if the United States were to do the same, some progress could be made. [37] When Mexico responded to these protests and others, some of them strongly worded, Helms commented: "All Latins are volatile people. Hence, I was not surprised at the volatile reaction."[38]

Mexican officials were particularly irritated by the testimonies of John Gavin, former United States ambassador to Mexico and United States Customs Commissioner William Von Raab. Both were highly critical of Mexico's antidrug efforts. Raab called Mexico's drug trade a "horror story, increasing logarithmically, and Mexico is doing nothing about it."[39] Gavin again raised the issue of the involvement of Mexican governors, arguing that "at least two" were "up to their elbows in the drug trade."[40] Part of the psychology behind Helms' exercises was noted by Lowenthal:

For the United States, it is natural to concentrate on Mexico, a prime and visible source of the narcotics traffic, right on the U.S. border. It is politically convenient to show that aggressive and effective measures are being taken to combat drug traders, and that these measures include vigorous activities in Mexico.[41]

During the hearings, the two presidents met to discuss the debt crisis, immigration and the drug trade. On the Mexican side, the Helms hearings were an embarrassment and there was a degree of confusion about whether this was an attack on Mexico by the Reagan administration. Part of the confusion stemmed from the differences in political systems. In Mexico, it would have been unthinkable that the Congress, usually a body subservient to the office of the president, make attacks on a visiting chief executive unless ordered to do so. As one member of the National Security Council commented: "The Mexicans were very confused about the whole situation, which, in some ways, was embarrassing for the President as well."[42]

Reagan and de la Madrid did agree to work together on the drug trade, with the latter pledging greater cooperation. In Mexico, a new antidrug campaign was launched during the meeting in Washington. The new operation involved twenty-five helicopters and a large crop-dusting plane (financed with United States aid) and targeted marijuana production in northern Mexico. Spraying was extensive and was intended to last through February to catch the 1987 opium poppy harvest. As one Mexican official noted of their campaign and the fact that it was conducted without United States personnel: "We Mexicans think that combating drug trafficking in the case of Mexico should continue to be carried out exclusively by the Mexican army and the Mexican police."[43] The idea of United States troops or police on Mexican soil would have been difficult to sell the Mexican people considering the history of United States involvement in Mexican affairs, ranging from annexation of substantial parts of the country such as Texas and California to the intervention of General Pershing.

The movement toward better relations with the United States on the drug issue were, however, quickly marred by a new incident. Even as the two heads of state met in Washington, police in Guadalajara detained a DEA agent, Victor Cortez, and tortured him. Though the agent was released, it did not help improve relations. Attorney General Edwin Meese protested to his counterpart, Attorney General Sergio Garcia Ramirez. Throughout the rest of 1986, the narcotics issue was a sore point between the two countries.

The Mexican government responded to North American pressure in a number of ways. It launched a public affairs campaign in Mexico and the United States that sought to project Mexico's "side of the story," The major points were that while Mexico did have problems with enforcement, the blame actually sat at the doorstep of the United States. The United States was, after all, the major market for Mexican drugs: if demand in the United States was not so high, then Mexican drug production would not be so high. Moreover, how did the United States expect Mexico to impose austerity programs, repay its external debt (mainly to United States) banks, and launch and sustain an effective war on drugs? To win a war on drugs, money had to be spent. The debt crisis reduced that money considerably. Moreover, it was understandable that there was corruption in the government and enforcement agencies. With the fall in the standard of living related to austerity programs and tight money policies, the incentive to cheat became higher. It was easy to earn more than a year's salary by looking the other way once or twice. All things considered, the Mexicans pointed the finger of blame at the United States. As President de la Madrid stated: "Not recognizing one's own problems and trying to find their roots in the problems of others is a human tendency. I have stated, and this is Mexican government policy, that drug trafficking is an international crime."[44]

While pointing the finger of blame at the United States for not controlling its addicts, the Mexicans did move on the drug trade in their country. In October 1986, a major antidrug campaign resulted in the arrest of the brother of a former governor of the State of Sonoro. Gilberto Ocana García was charged with drug trafficking in connection with the marijuana fields he owned. Moreover, the Mexican government made public its antinarcotics work over the past three years. According to Mexican sources, the Mexican army and navy and the attorney general's office assigned 45,000 men to the effort, 90 percent of the marijuana and poppy producing capacity was destroyed, and 18,792 people, both nationals and foreigners, were arrested.[45] In the three-year effort, the army lost 318 men, the navy 25, and the attorney general's office, 43.

One incident in particular was the November 1985 slaying of twenty-one Mexican policemen in southern Mexico by *narcotraficantes*. The police intercepted a major shipment of marijuana on land. A firefight ensued with the traffickers who were well-equipped. A number of police were killed in the fight, but the majority surrendered when they ran out of ammunition. They were then taken to a river where they were tortured and shot. Only a few police survived out of the original force. Edward J. Williams noted of the overall Mexican antinarcotics effort: "Though far from perfect, Mexico's efforts in the struggle reflect significant commitment. The United States has lost one agent to the Mexican drug mafia, but dozens of Mexican soldiers and policemen have been tortured and killed."[46]

## OF CORRUPTION AND VIOLENCE

There has been considerable debate over corruption in the Mexican government and violence linked to the drug trade. Accusations have been made, both in Mexico and in the United States, that drug-related corruption exists throughout the government. Mills strongly argued that the Cuban-American trafficker, Alberto Sicilia-Falcon who lived in Mexico and dominated the trade during the 1970s, had ties "right into the offices of *Gobernacíon*, a superagency functioning not only as a law enforcement unit but as the Mexican equivalent of the CIA."[47] Sicilia-Falcon also had extensive ties with officials in the PRI and a guerrilla chieftain fighting in the isolated, marijuana-rich mountains of the Sierra Madre del Sur between Acapulco and Mexico City. He traded guns for marijuana with the latter. Sicilia-Falcon was clearly a major player and his lifestyle was openly flamboyant and known to local and federal officials. It was only after years of United States pressure that he was brought to justice and sentenced. Even then, maintains Mills, certain Mexican officials sought to slow the judicial process and were obstructive.

In de la Madrid's administration, Mexico's law enforcement officials were underpaid, poorly regulated, and corruption was commonplace. Practices ranged from "protection" money for automobiles (small sums) to substantial amounts for "looking the other way." Mills accounts that on one occasion when Mexican officials did do their job and raided Sicilia-Falcon's residence, many of those involved were soon transferred to other less appealing duties, such as airplane watching.

One of the worst cases of corruption in the enforcement agencies was Arturo Durazo Moreno, the Chief of Police in Mexico City. Appointed by Lopez Portillo, Durazo Moreno had been the new president's bodyguard and the position was his reward. His apparently made good use of it to amass a personal fortune, including real estate in the United States. Not only did Durazo Moreno take bribes, he was also alleged to be a trafficker. Freemantle noted:

During his kinglike reign, Moreno amassed a fortune. Within his 3,000 Department for the Investigation and Prevention of Delinquency, he created a torturing, murdering vigilante squad estimated to have been responsible for at least twenty assassinations. Officially with a salary of only $1,000 a month, Moreno built two estates—one covering 600 acres near Acapulco, the other on the outskirts of Mexico City—valued at $15,000,000.[48]

When Portillo's tenure of office ended in December 1982, Durazo Moreno left the country. He quickly became one of Mexico's most wanted criminals, later being arrested in Puerto Rico and extradited.

The United States view of Mexico's enforcement (and political) system is epitomized by the following statement in a government report: "Corruption of Mexican police officials is well-documented and is essential to the smooth operation of the Mexican trafficking organizations."[49] Because of the growing clamor inside Mexico and United States pushiness over corruption, the de la Madrid government implemented some reforms and vowed to improve the situation. In an interview in July 1984, de la Madrid stated:

I cannot say that we have totally succeeded, far from it. In Mexico we have neglected the police situation for many years, indeed, for decades. We did not pay attention to the police; we did not recognize the role they should play in a civilized society, policemen were not motivated to embrace their work as a professional career and we allowed a great deal of corruption in the various corps. I must confess we are barely making a beginning in this task and the results as yet are not satisfactory, but I believe the Mexican people deserve a good legal, judicial and police system.[50]

Another element often overlooked in North America is the vulnerability of law enforcement officials to the drug trade's violence. Violence is an integral part of Mexican trafficking as members provide cultivators with semiautomatic and automatic weapons. To protect crops, informants are often brutally murdered, competitors raided, and law enforcement agents intimidated. Low pay for dangerous work and a lack of respect for the police as an occupational path in Mexico have hurt morale and opened the door to drug-related corruption. The debt crisis, with its budget cuts has not helped this situation.

The Camerena case brought the issue of government corruption to the fore. It was made public that traffickers dealt with the same high ranks of government as they had in the 1970s when Sicilia-Falcon was the drug kingpin. Under United States and domestic pressure, a few sacrificial lambs were cast from the fold, such as Comandante Pavon. Mills suggested that Caro Quintero and two others (Fonseca and Felix) were part of a much larger operation that involved other members of the federal government and that the question of who ordered Camerena's death went unanswered. To Mills, the answer lies in the PRI and its long rule: "During that rule, criminal participation in government had become pervasive and routine."[51] He also pointed to Echeverria and Lopez-Portillo (the latter went to live in Paris) amassing "hundreds of millions of dollars in criminal profits."[52] And, finally, not to blame Mexico entirely, Mills suggested that many Mexican (and non-Mexican) traffickers had ties to the CIA, which oftentimes protected them, in coordination with the Mexican intelligence community, as important sources of information concerning Central America. Hence, the emergence of a Gordian knot of greed, nationalist sensitivities, and national security.

## CONCLUSION

There have been three footnotes to the Camarena case. On 9 December 1987, the United States and Mexican governments signed a mutual legal assistance treaty, which provided a number of new areas of cooperation. One of the most significant new stipulations was the "voluntary" transferring of persons in custody for testimonial or identification purposes. This new agreement, which took several years to negotiate, did not extend to widening extradition powers between the two countries. This was soon made obvious.

In the second footnote to the Camarena case, nine men, including three former Mexican policemen, were indicted on January 6, 1988 in connection with the torture and murder of the DEA agent. The indictment was returned by a Federal grand jury in Los Angeles and accused two former police officers and three others, including drug baron Caro Quintero and his chief lieutenant René Martin Verdugo Urquidez, of direct involvement in Camarena's death.[53] Three of the suspects were in custody in the United States, with the rest in Mexico. Two of those in Mexico were still at large. Although the United States indicated that they wanted the extradition of those held in custody in Mexico, the prospects for that were not high as Mexican law permits extradition only in exceptional cases. Confirmation came on January 7, that Mexican and United States officials agreed that there would be no attempt to extradite Caro Quintero.

The third footnote was an indirect outcome of the Camarena case, but fits into United States frustration with the flow of drugs from Mexico. In April 1988, the United States Senate overwhelmingly approved economic sanctions against Mexico for failing to fully cooperate in U.S. antidrug efforts. This was the result of an earlier Senate vote (63 to 27) to reject President Reagan's certification of Mexico as complying with a 1986 law that threatens sanctions against any country that falls short in assisting the United States combat the drug trade. Decertification requires that the United States oppose new loans from international development banks and curtailment of foreign aid. Although Mexico receives no foreign aid (only anti-drug assistance of around $14 million), the debt crisis makes new loans crucial. The sad fact is that decertification could have equally negative effects on the United States' financial sector if Mexico is forced to default. According to the Federal Financial Institutions Examination Council, at year-end 1987 Mexico owed United States commercial banks $22.4 billion. While decertification has the potential to put more pressure on Mexico's ability to meet its external obligations, it could also cause further budget cuts in government spending, including enforcement agencies as well as further incentives for bribery and other forms of corruption. Decertification, moreover, has not helped create an atmosphere of cooperation between the two nations. Fortunately, the measure did not appear before Congress and did not become active policy. It remained an indication of U.S. discontent.

Alan Riding has commented: "Probably nowhere in the world do two countries as different as Mexico and the United States live side by side."[54] This fundamental difference between the two nations has clearly colored each country's perception of the drug trade and possible solutions. Mexico has long favored demand-side solutions, while pursuing supply-side interdiction, sometimes under duress. Mexicans often feel that the United States seeks to blame Mexico for the inflow of narcotics. On the other side of the border, Mexico's growing role in the drug trade in the late 1980s was met with charges of corruption and bureaucratic ineptitude. The solution to some was to go to the source; that is, take the fight to drug traders on their own turf. Considering Mexican nationalism, this was strongly resisted; there was little desire to have United States troops back on Mexican soil as once they come, they have a tendency to remain. At least, this was the way that some perceived it.

Cooperation between Mexico and the United States is highly desired if the drug trade is to be reduced in any discernable fashion. Unfortunately, the narcotics issue is one of many concerns that flood the agenda of Mexican-United States relations. Other issues, such as free trade, subsidization, immigration, Central America, and the debt crisis often claim greater attention. Narcotics come to the fore usually only after a major incident, which is indeed unfortunate as the "fireman" approach has a tendency to leave most parties in a state of great sensitivity.

## NOTES

1. *The New York Times*, September 9, 1969, p. 1.

2. Juan de Onis, "Mexican Farmers Discover Big Money in Grass," *The New York Times*, September 18, 1969, p. 1.

3. *The New York Times*, September 9, 1969, p. 9.

4. Ibid., p. 1.

5. Ibid.

6. Alan Riding, *Distant Neighbors: A Portrait of the Mexicans* (New York: Alfred A. Knopf, 1985), p. 337.

7. Juan de Onis, "Drug Watch on Mexico Adding to Latin Disillusion With Nixon," *The New York Times*, October 8, 1969, p. 17.

8. Abraham Lowenthal, *Partners in Conflict: The United States and Latin America* (Baltimore: The Johns Hopkins University Press, 1987), p. 87.

9. Ibid., p. 8.

10. For accounts on Mexico's debt crisis see Norman A. Bailey and Richard Cohen, *The Mexican Time Bomb* (New York: Priority Press Publications, 1987) and Roberto Newell G. and Luis Rubio, F., *Mexico's Dilemma: The Political Origins of Economic Crisis* (Boulder, Colorado: Westview Press, 1984).

11. Scott B. MacDonald, "Country Study: Mexico," *American Security Bank Country Study Series*, April 1987.

12. These are rough estimates reached from figures in The International Monetary Fund, *International Financial Statistics, November 1987* (Washington, D.C.: International Monetary Fund, November 1987), pp. 348–351.

13. Taken from selected passages from the address given by Gustavo Perticioli, Secretary of Finance and Public Credit, given at the Third Annual Meeting of National Banks, Guadalajara, Jallisco, Mexico, July 9, 1987, quoted in "Stability

for Growth," *Banamex: Review of the Economic Situation of Mexico* (Mexico City), Vol. 62, No. 740 (July 1987), p. 173.

14. For a recent article on this see Adolfo Aguilar Zinser, "Mexico: The Presidential Problem," *Foreign Policy* (Winter 1987–88), No. 69.

15. Jesús Yanéz Orozco, "The Fight Against Drug Trade," *Voices of Mexico*, September-November 1986, No. 1, p. 52.

16. Abraham Lowenthal, *Partners in Conflict*, p. 87.

17. President's Commission on Organized Crime, *America's Habit: Drug Abuse, Drug Trafficking, and Organized Crime* (Washington, D.C.: U.S. Government Printing Office, March 1986), pp. 109–110.

18. Ibid., p. 110.

19. *The Latin America Times*, December 1987, p. 12.

20. Ibid.

21. Jesús Yanéz Orozco, "Creative Smugglers," *Voices of Mexico*, September-November 1986, No. 1, p. 55.

22. Ibid.

23. "Mexico's Permanent Campaign Against Narcotics Trafficking," *Mexico Today*, May 1985, p. 5.

24. Jesús Yanez Orozco, "The Fight Against Drug Trade," *Voices of Mexico*, p. 56.

25. Ibid.

26. Jay Matthews, "Cocaine Seizures Up In California," *The Washington Post*, January 2, 1988, p. A3.

27. Brian Freemantle, *The Fix: Inside the World Drug Trade* (New York: Tom Doherty Associates, Inc., 1986), p. 151.

28. According to an account told to Freemantle from a top DEA aid, Mullen went to Mexico and began banging on desks to get some action. This was confirmed by Mullen in an interview with the author on January 6, 1988.

29. Mary Thornton, "Suspect in DEA Slaying Said to Live Well in Mexico," *The Washington Post*, February 22, 1986, p. A1.

30. James Mills, *The Underground Empire: Where Crime and Governments Embrace* (Garden City, New York: Doubleday & Company Inc., 1986), p. 1155.

31. Ibid.

32. Mary Thornton, "Suspect in DEA Slaying," *The Washington Post*, February 22, 1986, p. A4.

33. Mary Thornton, "A Murder at the Border of No-Man's Land," *The Washington Post*, April 13, 1986, p. A3.

34. Quoted in Thornton, "Mexico Is Top U.S. Source of Heroin," *The Washington Post*, February 22, 1986, p. A20.

35. Ibid.

36. Ibid.

37. David Gardner, "Mexico protests to US over drug trafficking claims," *The Financial Times*, May 15, 1987, p. 5.

38. Associated Press, "Helms Slates New Hearings on Mexico," *The Washington Post*, June 9, 1986, p. A6.

39. Op-Ed, "Mexico's Finest," *The New York Times*, August 20, 1986, p. A22.

40. Susan Benesch, "Gavin Links Top Mexicans To Narcotics," *The Washington Post*, June 27, 1986, p. A15.

41. Abraham Lowenthal, *Partners in Conflict*, pp. 87–88.

42. Comments made to author in Washington in 1986.

43. William Stockton, "Mexico's Drug Effort Will Also Be Home-Grown," *The New York Times*, August 17, 1986, p. 26.

44. Jesús Yanez Orozco, "The Fight Against Drug Trade," *Voices of Mexico*, Sept.-Nov. 1986, p. 52.

45. Ibid., p. 53.

46. Edward J. Williams, "The Implications of the Border for Mexican Policy and Mexican-United States Relations," in Roderic A. Camp (editor), *Mexico's Political Stability: The Next Five Years* (Boulder, Colorado: Westview Press, 1986), p. 222.

47. James Mills, *The Underground Empire*, p. 94.

48. Brian Freementle, *The Fix*, p. 149.

49. President's Commission on Organized Crime, *America's Habit*, p. 109.

50. "Mexico: An Exclusive Interview with Miguel de la Madrid," *Excelsior*, Mexico City, July 1984, p. 81.

51. James Mills, *The Underground Empire*, p. 1157.

52. Ibid.

53. Philip Shenon, "U.S. Charges 9 In Mexico of Drug Death," *The New York Times*, January 7, 1988, p. 1, and Jay Mathews, "Nine Indicted In '85 Slayings of DEA Agent," *The Washington Post*, January 7, 1988, p. A24.

54. Alan Riding, *Distant Neighbors*, p. xi.

# 6

# The Caribbean Producers: Jamaica and Belize

## INTRODUCTION

The growing influence of drug traffickers and marijuana producers in the 1980s has become a growing concern in Jamaica and Belize. These two Anglo-Caribbean countries were respectively the second and fourth largest sources of imported marijuana into the United States in 1984. In 1987, it was probable that Jamaica surpassed Colombia in terms of volume entering North American markets. Belize and Jamaica are integral parts of the Latin American drug trade, functioning as both producers and transshippers: marijuana is locally cultivated and exported and cocaine is transported through these countries. In Jamaica, marijuana, referred to as *ganja*, is the largest cash crop, possibly worth between $1–2 billion in annual returns, while the value of the annual marijuana crop in Belize is estimated at $350 million, well above the total for licit exports.[1]

The impact of the drug trade has been enormous in Jamaica and Belize. Marijuana use had been a traditional element, but cocaine has not, raising questions over rising addiction. Moreover, the local and foreign *narcotraficantes* operating in these countries have considerable firepower. Though it would be difficult to foresee either country deteriorate before a cocaine coup, as in the case of Bolivia in the early 1980s, the drug trade has become a serious challenge to the authority of the state and national security. In Jamaica, this challenge is greatly complicated by the long-term nature of the country's debt crisis and commodity dependence.

This chapter examines the drug trade in Jamaica and Belize. The first section provides the historical background of marijuana usage in Jamaica and the structure of production and exportation. The following sections discuss the role of the drug trade in Jamaican politics, its impact on United States relations and Belize's smaller, yet no less significant role in the drug trade.

## *GANJA* IN JAMAICA

*Ganja* usage has become part of the texture of Jamaican life. This is not to suggest that all Jamaicans use marijuana or that one, massive cloud of drug smoke overhangs the Caribbean island-state. The linkage between *ganja* and Jamaican history/culture commenced when marijuana was introduced by East Indians arriving to work the sugar plantations following the emancipation of the slaves in 1838. Since that time, it has steadily diffused to the Afro-Jamaican segments of the population and currently enjoys regular and frequent use throughout the working class.[2] Domestic cultivation was a logical offshoot from consumption, especially as Jamaica's climate is particularly hospitable to the crop capable of two harvests yearly.

Marijuana is produced throughout Jamaica. The following parishes have at one point or another have been known as production areas: St. Ann, St. Mary, St. Thomas, Westmoreland, St. Catherine, Clarendon, St. Elizabeth, Trelawny, Manchester, Hanover, and St. James. In the 1978–81 period, the DEA estimated that an average of 740–1,400 metric tons of marijuana were supplied to the United States market by Jamaica. By the 1980s cannabis had become the leading income earner for at least 6,000 Jamaican farmers and, according to one estimate, in 1982 there was a total of 19,000 acres under marijuana cultivation on the island.[3] As of 1985, the cannabis "narcodollar" contributed between $1 to $2 billion to the island's foreign exchange earnings, more than all other exports combined, including bauxite, sugar, and tourism.[4]

Drug smuggling as a major economic activity commenced in the 1950s and has continued ever since. Jamaican efforts to control *ganja*, however, date back to at least 1907 when the British government terminated the practice of supplying cannabis from India to the East Indian community in the Caribbean. Though the first penal restrictions were imposed in 1913, it was only in 1924 that cultivation was prohibited and the sale and possession were to be controlled by regulation of licences. Anyone who wanted to sell marijuana had to pay a duty of 10 pounds to the Treasury for a licence. This law was not enforced with any diligence until after the 1938 labor riots when the white planter elite associated *ganja*, Rastafarians, with the political instability.[5] The 1941 Amendment of the Dangerous Drugs Law incorporated the principle of mandatory imprisonment, which was used at times against the Rastas. Only in 1972 was the mandatory imprisonment clause dropped.

There are some questions about who is involved in Jamaica's *ganja* trade. The Rastafarians are often linked to the trade and related violence, which in many respects, is not an accurate assessment. Before proceeding further, it is necessary to explain who the Rastafarians are and what they believe in. Anita M. Waters described the basic tenets of belief of this socioreligious group:

> The Rastafarians are a largely unorganized group united only around a few central beliefs. First and foremost is the belief in the divinity of Haile Selassie. He is considered by some as the invincible man and the living God. . . . Rastifari is millenarian in the sense that Selassie is believed to be preparing Ethiopia for the repatriation of the Rastafarians and other African and non-African people. . . . Second, the Rastas believe that the Bible is the purloined history of the African race, taken by Europeans at the time of enslavement. . . . Third, the Old Testament history of the Israelites' captivity in Babylon is interpreted as prophecy of the period of African slavery and continuing Black poverty in the New World.[6]

Part of the Rastafari faith condoned the use of *ganja*. A sizeable number of Rastas are strict vegetarians and adhere to the dietary laws of the Bible. Along these lines, they smoke, eat, or drink *ganja*. It is smoked as cigarettes (called *splif* or *skilf*), through the waterpipe (referred to as the *huka*), drunk as a medicinal tea, or cooked with vegetables and eaten. Rastas argue that there is a Biblical justification for *ganja* use and cite the following passages: Genesis 1:12, 3:18; Exodus 10:12; and Psalms 104:14. To the Rastas, *ganja* is not a drug, but an herb. Drugs are alcohol, tobacco, and pork.

Typical Rasta cultivation of *ganja* in Jamaica in the pre–1960s was on a small scale and not a major commercial activity. Even now, in the late 1980s, many Rastas continue to cultivate small amounts of marijuana for their own personal use or to generate additional income to build up smallholdings and achieve a degree of self-sufficiency from the "Babylonian shitstem."[7] It was in the early 1960s that cannabis cultivation markedly shifted from domestic use to export markets. As Malyon noted: "Then, with the arrival of Western 'hippy' tourists, in particular Americans, the plant's economic potential as an export crop started to be realized."[8] By the mid–1960s, the export of *ganja* to the United States was in the process of becoming a highly organized, multimillion dollar industry. With the shift from small-scale production for domestic consumption to exports, marijuana cultivators in the isolated parts of the island increasingly became bold and, on occasion, stoned or sniped at police raiding parties. Organized crime, with networks that penetrated customs and immigration agencies in Jamaica and North America, provided outlets, money and probably, later in the 1960s, guns.[9] The emerging *ganja*-for-guns trade was given a tremendous boost in the late 1960s by United States-Mexican efforts against marijuana trafficking: the drop in Mexican marijuana in the United States market was met by increased supply of Jamaican *ganja*.

Jamaican society in the 1960s was gradually penetrated by the drug trade, as violence, characterized by gang warfare in major population centers like Kingston, threatened the established order. Corruption spread in government and enforcement agencies and linkages developed between the more influential traffickers and minor politicians. Moreover, Jamaica's fledgling gun culture quickly overlapped into the political realm as the high level of unemployment supplied a small army of dissatisfied youth linked to either a criminal gang or a gang linked to one of the island's major political parties, the Jamaican Labour Party (JLP) or Peoples National Party (PNP). These political gangs often supplied bodyguards and sought to intimidate members of the opposition.

The rise of gangs with names such as Skull, Viking, and Dirty Dozen, reflected an angry subculture of youth answering to the pseudonym "Rude Bowy."[10] Many were employed in the *ganja* trade as enforcers. The negative image of Rastas in Jamaican society was reinforced by many of the Rude Bowys wearing their hair in dreadlocks. The violence of the *ganja* trade was only worsened by intimidation tactics and the blurring of the border between criminal activities and political competition. Both Michael Manley, leader of the PNP, and Pearnel Charles, then JLP leader, surrounding themselves with "bad men" recruited from the ranks of the unemployed. The 1960s were one of the country's most violent periods and the size of the drug industry and the vested interests which related to it, help explain part of that political and criminal violence.[11]

Manley's victory in 1972 brought with it the expectation that there would be a decriminalization of marijuana and a disarming of the Rude Bowys. Support for Manley had come from the Rasta community and small *ganja* farmers. Therefore expectations were high that the new PNP government would implement a more liberal code vis-a-vis marijuana production. One of the first acts of the Manley administration was the revoking of the mandatory eighteen-month sentence for the possession and commerce of cannabis. A "Gun Court" was also established to bring under control the almost rampant use of firearms in Jamaican society.

The PNP's move to bring order into society ran headlong into a booming *ganja* trade. Violent crime rose as rival gangs sought to eliminate each other over the increasingly lucrative market. By 1974, the *ganja* trade had grown to a value of $400 million annually.[12] Government crackdowns were largely ineffectual and traffickers grew increasingly bolder. This was exemplified by the assassination attempt in mid–1974 on Jamaican Minister of National Security and Justice Eli Matalon who was in Miami discussing narcotics issues with United States officials. The scope of the trade as a problem had moved well beyond the control of the Jamaican government. This, in turn, caused tenser relations with a United States already concerned at the growing marijuana inflow.

The governments of President Nixon and Prime Minister Manley agreed to cooperate against the drug trade in "Operation Buccaneer." The major objective was to disrupt the trade in cannabis between the two countries by interdiction on the high seas and crop eradication. Full-scale military operations in the rural areas, supported by United States helicopters and fixed-wing aircraft, proceeded in a damaging search-and-destroy campaign. While this crackdown did have a positive impact on reducing the scope of the *ganja* trade, it also bound working class users and cultivators with the big dealers in their defiance of the law.[13] Although Operation Buccaneer briefly reduced the flow of cannabis northwards, enforcement measures lagged in the late 1970s in large part because of the economic recession. By Seaga's victory in 1980, the trade in marijuana was estimated to have a yearly value of $1–2 billion.[14]

In the 1980s, Jamaica's marijuana production increased substantially because of greater demand in North America and Colombian eradication efforts. By 1984, the price of Jamaican marijuana had dropped by 50 percent since 1982, suggesting a greater availability. One source indicated that actual production went from 2,460 metric tons in 1982 to 1,559–2,909 metric tons in 1985.[15]

## THE ETHIOPIAN ZION COPTIC CHURCH

While there were a number of gangs involved in the drug trade in Jamaica in the late 1970s and 1980s, none has been as well-known and bizarre as the Ethiopian Zion Coptic Church. Most Jamaican traffickers have been less highly organized than their Colombian and Mexican counterparts. Not so with the Ethiopian Zion Coptic Church. According to DEA sources, the Ethiopian Zion Coptic Church is clearly one of the major forces in the trade. Led by a convicted marijuana trafficker, Keith Gordan (also known as Edmund Gordan), the Church is wealthy, powerful, and has operations stretching from Florida to Colombia. Freemantle noted:

From the Jamaican capital, Kingston, the church runs a vast complex of trucking companies, auto parts suppliers, supermarkets and furniture stores. It also has airstrips at Byran Castel, Trelawny, and Alim and it is believed to own seven thousand acres of prime agricultural—marijuana-growing—land in Colombia. But its principal product is the highly prized and potent sinsemilla.[16]

What is bizarre about the Ethiopian Zion Coptic Church? Though nobody wants to claim it, one school of thought has portrayed it as an agent of the United States government established to subvert the Manley government in the late 1970s.[17] At the same time, the DEA has identified them as a criminal organization active in the drug trade in the United States and Caribbean. What is certain is that the Church has considerable influence in Jamaica and is probably a major force in the island's *ganja* trade. What has made the Church such an oddity is its founding beliefs. Founded in 1975, the Church advocates "the belief in the Bible, the Moral Laws of God, the Fatherhood of God and the Brotherhood of Man to safeguard and transmit to prosperity the purity and righteousness of the precepts and teachings as taught by them."[18] The very odd element of all this was that Zion Coptics, predominately white Americans, claimed they were Rastafari and came to international attention for the defense of the right to smoke and use marijuana as the Church's "holy sacrament." While that helped endear them among some of the Rasta community, the idea of "white Rastas" appeared to others as a contradiction in terms. Campbell noted:

The Coptics have, in the process of linking themselves with local blacks, introduced the concept that "white Americans" could be Rastas, calling into question one of the fundamental tenets of Rastifari that 'the Rasta is one who never forgets that he is African.' From their headquarters in Star Island, in Florida, USA, these capitalists, who have found it convenient to wear the cover of Rasta, set out to acquire land and followers in Jamaica so that they could further their accumulations.[19]

It therefore appeared to some Jamaicans that the Church was a front organization for whites wishing to deal in *ganja*. It was also felt that Gordon, a black Jamaican, was only a figurehead to appease the locals. The Coptics expanded their operations during the Manley years, becoming a powerful economic force. In 1980, when the International Monetary Fund had withdrawn all funding and credit and the country was exceedingly short of foreign exchange, it was alleged that the Church-dominated *ganja* trade kept the economy afloat. Only a few months later shortly after Seaga was elected he alluded to the Church's influence: "The *ganja* trade in the last several months was virtually keeping the economy afloat."[20] By 1981, the Ethiopian Zion Coptic Church was one of the largest private landowners in the country, leading the *Daily Gleaner* in 1981 to call it "a country within Jamaica."

In the United States, where the Church owns a mansion on Star Island paid for by $270,000 in cash, its activities have been curtailed. On a Church-owned Florida farm, ten tons of cannabis were siezed and a number of members were arrested. Others have served time in prison on charges of marijuana importation, trafficking, and conspiracy charges involving two specific transactions that amounted to 33.5 tons and unloading multiton quantities of cannabis on six occasions.[21] In addition, they were charged with "bribing of Jamaican military officers to obtain information as to the location and planning of the Jamaican Coast Guard and Defense Force."

Although the Ethiopian Zion Coptic Church has not fared well in the United States, it has found fertile soil in Jamaica. The change in government from the democratic socialist Manley to the pro-capitalist Seaga did little to change circumstances. Jamaica's dire economic conditions—consecutive years of contraction or near-stagnation in the late 1970s and a heavy external debt burden of $1.5 billion (in 1980)—made Seaga less than enthusiastic about pursuing drug traffickers, especially those who were responsible for large capital infusions and employment. In a sense, there was a danger that organizations like the Church, if attacked by the government, would cease to be almost essential sources of foreign exchange. A Coptic Church member explained:

The Seaga government hasn't really persecuted us at all in Jamaica. The government's attitude is that *ganja* is better than Communism. If it fights *ganja* too hard, then people will become antagonistic and turn to Communism, that's the other party, Michael Manley's party. So they prefer *ganja* to grow.[22]

Earlier in 1980, Seaga had stated the question of dealing with drugs in Jamaica was not one of eradication of the marijuana crop, but its legalization. Legalization would "bring the flow of several hundred million dollars in this parallel market through the official channels and therefore have it count as part of our foreign exchange."[23] He also noted that medical reports did not conclusively prove marijuana usage harmful and that legalization would eliminate other problems such as corruption and make gun smuggling more difficult. This line of reasoning and the relatively lax nature of drug enforcement were undoubtedly welcomed by the Ethiopian Zion Coptic Church. At the same time, Seaga's lack of effort against the drug trade had ramifications with Washington, his country's major source of external financial assistance.

## GETTING MR. SEAGA'S ATTENTION

The rise of the $1–2 billion marijuana trade in nearby Jamaica did not go unnoticed in the United States. Putting pressure on Seaga, however, posed problems. Relations with Jamaica under Manley had deteriorated considerably due to differences over the management of the country's external debt and the conduct of relations with Cuba. It was no mistake that Seaga was the first foreign head of state to visit the newly installed President Reagan in 1980. Both men shared an antipathy towards Communism and a desire to make Jamaica a show piece of what United States-aided democratic-capitalism could achieve. In return, Seaga was a firm advocate of the West in Caribbean affairs, supporting the United States-led intervention in Grenada in October 1983. That same year, Jamaica surpassed Mexico as the second major source of imported marijuana in the United States, holding 13 percent of the market to Colombia's 59 percent and Mexico's 9 percent.[24] There was also concern about the transshipment of cocaine from South America through Jamaica.

In 1984, the United States government began to bring pressure to bear on Seaga to do something about the drug trade. His response to the possibility that United States aid could be reduced unless action was taken was: "if you're going to analyze Jamaica's problems at any depth at this stage, you are going to run into the fact that this huge traffic is going on—which you may not consider to be to the advantage of your country [i.e., the USA]- and you are going to raise that question, and I in turn am going to have to say, well, it's keeping us alive. How else do we get kept alive?"[25]

Seaga had made some motions to address the drug situation. In the fall of 1983 the growing consumption of cocaine had led him to support the creation of the National Council on Drug Abuse. In 1984, promises were made to improve control of the country's fifty to seventy airfields. Seaga also announced plans to tax J$117 million in income tax from twenty-eight of the island's alleged marijuana traffickers.[26] Though there was supposedly a plot to murder the prime minister, no one was arrested and little else was reported on the tax campaign. What was done, however, was the eradication of part of the country's marijuana crop. In 1986, 7,160 acres of the weed were reported destroyed.[27]

In 1986 and 1987, Jamaica was confronted by a rising level of violent crime that threatened to damage the country's reputation as a tourist resort. Part of this crime was linked to the drug trade. In 1986, some 782 foreign individuals were held in Jamaica for drug offenses.[28] In response to the increasing use of his country as a transshipment point, Seaga took a radical step in October 1987 when he announced that the Jamaican Defense Force would shoot down any aircraft that failed to identify itself and refused to land.[29] While this caused a brief sensation, it was soon revealed that Jamaica did not have the surface-to-air missiles needed for such an operation. Seaga also outlined other measures, which were more realistic. These included a blockade of isolated airstrips, a barring of people who were convicted of drug offenses from re-entering the country, and a sharp increase in fines for trading and possession of drugs.

In the late 1980s, Jamaica continues to have a thriving drug trade and many of its principals remain active. Part of the problem remains the lack of political will to tackle the problem as the trade has linkages throughout the country's political and economic structure. Though difficult to prove, there have been allegations that members of the ruling JLP have been involved in the cocaine trade, while members of the PNP maintain closer ties to the *ganja* traders. Whatever the case, the drug trade is an important force in Jamaica's development and its influence is beginning to spread further in the United States. One of the newest developments has been the spread of the Jamaican drug mafia into the United States. In 1987 and 1988, there were a number of drug-related murders in the greater Washington, D.C. area. In particular, the January 1988 murder of five Jamaicans in Landover, Maryland raised the issue of the emergence of Jamaican drug gangs moving into the region, seeking to gain control. Like the Colombians and Mexicans, Jamaican gangs have had a penchant for executionlike violence and retaliation.

## THE RELATIONSHIP BETWEEN DEBT AND DRUGS

In the late 1970s when the drug trade expanded considerably, part of the attraction was the seemingly easy money to be gained at a time of prolonged economic crisis. The full scope of the drug problem cannot be understood without some background of the downturn in the country's financial picture in the mid–1970s. Jamaica has traditionally been a commodity-oriented economy. Throughout the sixteenth and seventeenth centuries, sugar was the locomotive that drove the economy. In the eighteenth century sugar began its long decline and it was only in the midtwentieth century that bauxite emerged as a more important sector. Tourism also developed as a significant source of revenues. Jamaican development, however, proved to be delicate: when oil prices increased in the 1973–74 period, the economy struggled to regroup. At the same time, bauxite prices rose and fell. By the second oil shock in 1979, the Jamaican economy had not yet recovered. Inflation was out of control and the country's politics were characterized by militancy and a preoccupation with protest politics and the making of demands on the society for more justice and opportunity for the poor.[30] The seemingly intractable economic crisis and the inability of the Manley administration to come to grips with the myriad problems, many of which were beyond its jurisdiction, led to a pattern of demoralization, political apathy and, in the word of Carl Stone, a "withdrawal into cynicism and hopelessness as many lost faith in political causes and lowered their expectations for benefits from the system and expected less from political leaders."[31] This shift was reinforced by the erosion in the GDP per capita income which fell from $2,259 in 1970 to $1,814 in 1980 (and $1,701 in 1985).[32]

Jamaica, like many nations in Latin America and the Caribbean, had opted to borrow from foreign creditors during the seventies. It was felt that these adverse international circumstances were temporary and that the country's economic development would resume to a upward path of expansion. Unfortunately, this was not the case. Jamaica's external debt (disbursed and outstanding) grew from $159.6 million in 1970 to $1.5 billion in 1981 and many of the negative trends did not fade, but became worse.[33] Austerity programs were implemented and with those came a rise in political violence and an attraction to other means of income outside the licit economy, such as that of drugs.

The "prudence" of both the Manley and Seaga governments in the late 1970s and early 1980s in leaving the drug trade alone was due to the dangerously low level of foreign exchange reserves. These reserves were a little over $30 million in 1976 and 1977, less than a month's coverage of imports.[34] Though the year-end figures improved in 1978 and 1979, they continued to be perilously low, greatly constricting the government's ability to meet its international obligations. In the first months of 1980, the situation reached a critical point as Manley broke relations with the International Monetary Fund and there was no relief at hand. Reserves almost disappeared and probably would have with the exception of the inflow of drug money. This made Seaga comment that the economy was sustained through this period only because the *ganja* trade played such an important role. The newly elected Prime Minister stated:

It supplied black market dollars which were then used by industrialists and other persons in the economy who wanted to import raw materials for which they could not get Bank of Jamaica dollars. On that basis they were able to avert a lot of closures and substantial lay-offs.[35]

Jamaica in the mid–1980s has undergone a long-term economic re-structuring, which unfortunately is not over. There have been improvements and a shift away from a dependence on the export of bauxite. However, as long as the economy continues to have structural problems, the temptation to allow the *ganja* trade a relatively unrestricted flow is inviting. It not only helps circulate capital throughout the economy, but also helps strengthen the country's ability to meet its foreign repayment obligations. In this respect, Jamaica's debt problem (over $4 billion in 1988) is very much interlinked to the drug trade and where the Jamaican government should cut the Gordian knot remains unanswered.

## BELIZE

Belize, formerly British Honduras, is a small country in Central America, slightly larger than the state of Massachusetts. Its population of 168,000 is divided between an Afro-Creole segment (51 percent), mestizo (22 percent), Amerindian (19 percent), and the rest is mixed. Belize has had a stable path of political development, despite the fact that neighboring Guatemala claims two-thirds of the country. This delayed independence from the United Kingdom until 1981 and has been the major reason for the maintenance of a British garrison in the country. The political system has been democratic and not marred by the violence of the surrounding region. However, there has been some concern in the 1980s that the drug trade has brought a violent element into Belize's political life.[36]

Major marijuana cultivation in Belize began in the 1960s and has been managed in part by North Americans. By the early 1980s, cannabis from that nation had gained fourth place in the United States market. However, there have also been local elements involved in both the cultivation of marijuana and the transshipment of cocaine. In 1984, a cocaine smuggling ring involving Belizeans was broken up in Miami. It operated from Colombia to Miami through Belize International Airport and had the alleged involvement of the assistant superintendent of police and manager of the airport. Another case involved the former Minister of Energy and Communications Eligio Briceno, who was arrested in Miami for conspiracy to supply 5,000 pounds of cannabis a month to contacts in the United States.

The government came under pressure by the United States to do something about illegal production. The Belizean government responded by having the Belize Defense Force and police conduct search and destroy missions as well as conducting chemical warfare on the crop with paraquat spray. In 1982 and 1983, fields were sprayed through parts of the country. This was done with the assistance of the United States and the Mexican governments. The result was that more than three thousand plantations covering an area of 14,400 acres were destroyed, arrests were made, drug laws were stiffened.[37]

In 1984, the spraying campaign was halted by the People's United Party (PUP) government of Prime Minister George Price. The spraying campaign was unpopular with most of the population for two primary reasons. First and foremost, the spraying was conducted around food crops and the poison had a tendency to creep into the ecosystem, eventually coming out in the food. Farmers and ecologists complained vocally about this. Secondly, many of the marijuana producers were said to have ties to both of the country's parties and it was thought that halting spraying was done to help the PUP remain in office.

At the same time, there was a feeling within the PUP government that the United States used pressure to make certain the drug trade remained under the gun. Alma H. Young noted: "Critics charged that the spraying was done to appease the United States because Caribbean Basin Initiative rules stipulate that the United States may withhold aid to those countries that do not do the maximum to stamp out the drug trade."[38] Along these lines, it was known that United States officials were irritated that that PUP government stopped spraying in 1983 while the country prepared for the elections. Caught on one hand with the unpopularity of spraying and yet aware of the clout of the United States in terms of economic assistance, the Price government found a compromise in having the security forces conduct search and destroy missions. The north, where most of the marijuana was cultivated, was particularly hard hit. Moreover, the same region of the country was struggling economically because of the closure of the Tate and Lyle sugar factory and the reductions in the United States sugar quotas for Belize. Many in the sugar-producing north found marijuana a good second crop.

The problem of drug eradication became part of the political campaign between Price's PUP and the opposition United Democratic Party (UDP). The UDP, led by Manuel Esquivel, clearly benefitted from voter dissatisfaction with the spraying as well as other issues, such as economic management in their electoral victory in 1984. On April 24, 1984, the new prime minister expressed the view that drug trafficking in Belize was more pernicious than the chemical spraying of marijuana fields.[39] Consequently, the UDP government has continued to support eradication measures as well as the maintenance of the British garrison of 2,000 soldiers and four Harrier Jump Jets. The former reduces the export of the crop to the United States, a major source of financial and developmental assistance. The latter guarantees a degree of stability and a substantial counterweight to well-equipped *narcotraficantes* using Belize as a transshipment point.

Considering that the country's economic resources are limited, any expenditure on high-tech weapons would be a substantial sacrifice to other programs, such as infrastructure development. The following comment by Police Commissioner Maxwell Samuels in February 1986 indicates the scope of the problem for Belizean enforcement: "the police, despite some of the shortcomings, have been doing a very good job within our limited resources."[40] As in Mexico and other nations, the fundamental problem remains limited resources.

There have been other offshoots of the drug trade in Belize. One of the more pressing concerns is the danger of arming the country's society, much as has occurred in Jamaica in the 1960s and 1970s. There was an incident in 1984 in which two members of the Belize Defense Force (BDF) shot innocent citizens, one fatally, during an antidrug operation. The two soldiers were convicted, but concern remained that parts of the country could become too dependent on the BDF to maintain law and order. Alma Young commented: "Roadblocks in the north have become commonplace, as soldiers search for drugs passing through the country. Increasing numbers of citizens have lodged complaints of brutality against BDF soldiers."[41]

Belize's concern about the drug trade provided the incentive to host a regional narcotics conference during the last week of March and early April, 1987. The conference, attended by delegates from twenty-six nations, was welcomed by Prime Minister Esquivél. The Belizean leader used the occasion to criticize the United States, which had diminished antinarcotics assistance at the same time it had reduced the potential for legitimate trade with the Caribbean countries (i.e., sugar quotas).[42] In a sense, United States protectionism in the sugar industry continued to be a factor in the expansion of drug trafficking in Belize, a country dependent upon that commodity as a major income earner. This had created problems in the rural areas that were the most dependent on sugar exports and where the standard of living was not as high.

Belize is an ideal nation for drug traffickers to operate. With a junglelike terrain and sparse settlement, it has a number of isolated airstrips that make easy pitstops for pilots flying from South America to North America. Moreover, the terrain of the country makes it difficult to patrol and the government lacks adequate resources to fully enforce drug laws throughout its domain. The British presence does function as a deterrent against the nation from being challenged in the same fashion that the *narcotraficantes* challenge the state's authority and legitimacy in Bolivia. There is no drug-insurgency nexus that is active, but many of the foundations for such a development exist throughout the surrounding region, and could conceivably overlap in the future, especially if the British presence ends.

## CONCLUSION

Jamaica and Belize share many of the same problems as their South American neighbors in regard to the drug trade. The question increasingly looms, will the Jamaican and Belizean governments have the capabilities on their own to confront the almost all-pervasive nature of the trade? Although the Jamaican government seized 1,200 pounds of cocaine in 1986 and the United States had provided $2.6 million for marijuana eradication, the scope of the trade appears to be expanding, not contracting.[43] The question of political will, therefore, is essential in any solution to the problem. Entangled with these issues is the role of *ganja* in society. Should marijuana be legalized and cocaine cracked down on? Can Jamaica afford to uproot the *ganja* industry in context to the impact it will have on its balance of payments and unemployment picture? It is likely that the drug problem, in terms of its threat to national security and societal ill-effects, will continue to worsen in both countries. The drug trade is clearly beyond the capacity of both nations, and outside assistance is essential. In Belize the situation is probably under better control because of the British presence. Does Jamaica need such a presence or outside assistance? These are delicate questions, touching upon national sentiments and future societal development. As in Bolivia, Colombia and Peru, the adjustment away from drug dependency will be difficult.

## NOTES

1. Horace Campbell, *Rasta and Resistance: From Marcus Garvey to Walter Rodney* (Trenton, New Jersey: New Africa Press, 1987), p. 112, and Tim Malyon, "Love Seeds and Cash Crops: The Cannabis Commodity Market," in Anthony Henman, Roger Lewis, and Tim Malyon (editors), *Big Deal: The Politics of the Illicit Drugs Business* (London: Pluto Press, 1985), p. 63.

2. Melanie Creagan Dreher, *Working Men and Ganja: Marijuana Use in Rural Jamaica* (Philadelphia: Institute for the Study of Human Issues, Inc., 1982), p. 1.

3. Brian Freemantle, *The Fix: Inside the World Drug Trade* (New York: Tom Doherty Associates, Inc., 1986), p. 264.

4. Tim Malyon, "Love Seeds and Cash Crops," Henman, Lewis, and Malyon, editors, *Big Deal*, p. 64.

5. Horace Campbell, *Rasta and Resistance*, p. 108.

6. Anita W. Waters, *Race, Class, and Political Symbols: Rastafari and Reggae in Jamaican Politics* (New Brunswick, New Jersey: Transaction Books, 1985), pp. 47–48.

7. Tim Malyon, "Love Seeds and Cash Crops," in Henman, Lewis, and Malyon (editors), *Big Deal*, p. 77.

8. Ibid.

9. Terry Lacey, *Violence and Politics in Jamaica 1960–70: Internal Security in a Developing Country* (Totowa, New Jersey: Frank Cass and Company Limited, 1977), p. 25.

10. Horace Campbell, *Rasta and Resistance*, p. 111.

11. Terry Lacey, *Violence and Politics in Jamaica 1960–70*, p. 160.

12. Horace Campbell, *Rastas and Resistance*, p. 112.

13. Ibid., p. 114.

14. Ibid., p. 112.

15. General Paul F. Gorman, "Illegal Drugs and US Security," in The President's Commission on Organized Crime, *America's Habit: Drug Abuse, Drug Trafficking, and Organized Crime* (Washington, D.C.: U.S. Government Printing Office, March 1986), p. 21.

16. Brian Freemantle, *The Fix*, p. 264.

17. Horace Campbell, *Rastas and Resistance*, pp. 115–118.

18. Quoted in *The Jamaica Gazette Extraordinary*, July 24, 1975.

19. Horace Campbell, *Rastas and Resistance*, p. 115.

20. Quoted in Malyon, "Love Seeds and Cash Crops," in Henman, Lewis, and Malyon, (editors), *Big Deal*, p. 64.

21. Ibid., pp. 82–83.

22. Ibid., p. 83.

23. Ibid.

24. Joseph B. Treaster, "Jamaica, Close U.S. Ally, Does Little to Halt Drugs," *The New York Times*, September 10, 1984, p. A12.

25. Tim Malyon, "Love Seeds and Cash Crops," in Henman, Lewis, and Malyon (editors), *Big Deal*, pp. 84–85.

26. Canute James, "Jamaica puts the tax squeeze on alleged marijuana traffickers," *The Financial Times*, October 24, 1984, p. 4.

27. *Latin America Regional Report Caribbean*, November 5, 1987, p. 3.

28. *Federal Broadcast Information Service*, September 30, 1987, p. 7.

29. *Latin America Regional Report Caribbean*, November 5, 1987, p. 7.

30. Carl Stone, *Class, State and Democracy in Jamaica* (New York: Praeger Publishers, 1986), p. xiii.

31. Ibid.

32. Inter-American Development Bank, *Economic and Social Progress in Latin American 1986 Report* (Washington, D.C.: Inter-American Development Bank, 1986), p. 394.

33. World Bank, *World Debt Tables: External Debt of Developing Countries 1985– 86 Edition* (Washington, D.C.: World Bank, 1986), p. 322.

34. International Monetary Fund, *International Financial Statistics Yearbook 1987* (Washington, D.C.: International Monetary Fund, 1987), pp. 420–421.

35. Tim Malyon, "Love Seeds and Cash Crops," in Henman, Lewis and Malyon (editors), *Big Deal*, p. 64.

36. Most of the information on Belize in this section came from the following sources: United States, Congress, House, Committee on Foreign Affairs and task Force on International Narcotics Control, *Narcotics Production and Transshipments in Belize and Central America* (Washington, D.C.: Government Printing Office, 1985).

37. Alma H. Young, "The Central America Crisis and Its Impact on Belize," in Alma H. Young and Dion E. Phillips (editors), *Militarization in the Non-Hispanic Caribbean* (Boulder, Colorado: Lyne Rienner Publishers, Inc., 1986), p. 150.

38. Ibid.

39. Ibid., p. 156.

40. "Is Violent Crime on the Increase?," *The New Belize*, February 1986, p. 15.

41. Alma Young, "The Central American Crisis," in *Militarization in the Non-Hispanic Caribbean*, p. 151.

42. Bruce Zagaris, "Belize Hosts Regional Narcotics Conference," *International Law Reporter*, Vol. 3, Issue 6 (June 1987), p. 177.

43. Donna Priest, "Caribbean is big supplier of US drugs," *The Washington Post*, February 23, 1988, p. A10.

# 7

# The Transit States

## INTRODUCTION: THE TRANSPORTATION-LAUNDERING NEXUS

This chapter focuses on the "transit states" and the "transportation-laundering nexus." Transit states are defined as those nations that are not necessarily producers of any major narcotic, but function as "pit stops" for traders. A particular state may serve as a base of operations to set up the deal, for aircraft or ship refueling, and for the recruitment of personnel required for such activities and protection. In addition, a number of transit states have the facilities for the laundering of "hot" money. Hence, the term—transportation-laundering nexus." This chapter will not examine either Belize and Jamaica nor Cuba and Nicaragua as these countries are discussed at greater length elsewhere in the book.

How is hot money laundered and is it difficult for law enforcement agencies to track? Though banking secrecy laws were tightened in the late 1980s, there were problems at the beginning of the decade. This was reflected by the testimony of United States Internal Revenue Service special agent Raul Dearmas.

Let us assume the domestic narcotics trafficker buys 100,000 pounds of marijuana. He pays $200 a pound. He would then get a profit of approximately $100 pound. The money will come to him little by little. At one point in time, he will have accumulated millions of dollars. So what can he do with that money? By creation of offshore operations, he is able then to buy legitimate businesses in this country and is able to invest in other businesses outside of this country. He is able to bring some of his narcotics profits back into the banking system by using these offshore banks and offshore corporations. We have specific cases in which individuals, one individual has formed 12 corporations in Panama, Caymans, Netherlands Antilles, Bahamas and . . . an island off the coast of Great Britain, which I never knew they were using that island as an offshore, but through that corporation, he channeled, he was able to channel back into the United States $3 million in currency from 1980 through December 1981.[1]

The major problem confronting enforcement agencies in the detection of the flow of hot money back into the United States were secrecy laws that were oriented to protect the investor. In one particular tax haven, the foreign investor purchased a shell corporation.[2] Then, in the name of the corporation, the investor deposits money in a bank authorized to do business with foreigners. If the investor was a North American, then his "partners" could be *narcotraficantes* from any number of other countries. Under the protection of the haven's secrecy laws, the corporation can transfer the money to the local branch of a large international bank, such as Citibank, Chemical, or Midland. Money is then borrowed from the branch in the name of another corporation. The result of this elaborate route is that the records of the bank in the United States fail to disclose what has happened because they reflect only a deposit by one company and a loan to another company that investigators cannot identify or trace. Though the United States put considerable pressure on a number of nations, such as Bermuda and the Cayman Islands, to tighten their rules concerning capital origination, money continues to be laundered in other fashions. Moreover, the heavy pressure used to bring Caribbean nations into a new tax treaty have had considerable political ripples, as many nations, such as the Bahamas, greatly resented United States pressure. Countries like the Netherlands Antilles have economies highly dependent on offshore banking and ongoing United States efforts to reduce the scope of operations threaten economic development and future political stability.

An often overlooked part of the debate about offshore banking and drugs has been the role of International Banking Facilities (IBFs) in the United States. IBFs were activated in December 1981 with the intention of making the United States banking sector more competitive in attracting offshore funds. IBFs are vehicles that enable bank offices in the United States to accept time deposits from non-United States residents free of reserve requirements and of interest-rate ceilings and also to lend to nonresidents not subject to most local (but not federal) income taxes.[3] By mid–1983, more than 400 banking institutions had established these vehicles with total assets of about $200 billion and this brought IBFs into the debate on the transportation-laundering nexus.[4] It is felt in the Caribbean that while the United States criticizes other countries for money laundering, the United States has the same problem of monitoring capital flows in its IBFs. United States efforts for greater information on banking secrecy in the Caribbean and elsewhere have therefore become entangled in the issue of IBFs.

The combination of drug trading and money laundering, as well as the legal side of international offshore banking, have been important international conduits of capital for a number of nations examined in this chapter. That capital has helped each nation's development in terms of economic expansion, employment generation, and raising wages. There has also been a downside: political corruption, problems of domestic addiction, rising crime rates, and, in certain cases, political instability. And, without a doubt, the transportation-laundering nexus has brought the United States into a test of political wills with a number of its allies in the 1980s and probably was a factor in the reelection of Lyndon Pindling in the Bahamian general elections of 1987. The United States antidrug effort has also been used by General Manuel Noriega, Panama's military strongman, who came under intense domestic pressure in 1987 due to his increasingly publicized involvement in drugs and arms trafficking, money laundering, and the September 1985 assassination of Dr. Hugo Spadafora.

The transit states are an important element in the Latin American drug trade. Without the use of the Caribbean's and Central America's bases, penetration of the United States and Canadian markets would be much more difficult. In addition to functioning as pitstops to the Colombians, the Caribbean populations are increasingly able to provide networks of friends and family in North America. One indication of this was the movement of Jamaican criminal groups into the Washington, D.C. drug trade in 1987. Though this does appear to be a trend, one needs to be careful in linking various ethnic groups to the drug trade as the criminal element usually represents a very small percentage of individuals from a particular country.

## THE POLLUTION OF A SOCIETY: THE BAHAMAS

The Bahamas is an archipelago of some 700 islands, about the size of Connecticut and covers some 36,098 square miles. The society is 85 percent black and 15 percent white, and literacy is close to 90 percent. In the late 1980s, the Bahamas has one of the highest standards of living in the Caribbean and Latin America. Unlike many of its neighbors, it lacks an external debt problem and has weathered most global economic storms relatively well. One of the main reasons for the Bahamas ability to ride global recessions and waves of protectionism has been the Latin American drug trade. According to both North American and Bahamian sources, the drug trade has become an important part of the island-state's economy and has gradually caused a degree of societal deterioration.

The Bahamas have flourished as part of the transit system in the Latin

American drug trade for several reasons: its proximity to the United States; the archipelago nature of its geography that makes enforcement difficult; and the structure of its banking system.[5] Since independence in 1973, the Bahamas aggressively pursued the development of offshore banking and international financial services. In the late 1980s, it continued to be the leading financial Caribbean offshore center, ahead of the Cayman Islands and Panama.[6] Consequently, the banking sector was an important part of the economy. Any attacks upon it, such as demands by other governments about Bahamian clients, were perceived as a threat not just to the banking system, but to the nation's overall economic well-being. As *The Latin American Times* noted: "Preservation of secrecy is widely held by the government and the business community to remain absolutely critical for the continued success and growth of the Bahamas as a leading international financial centre."[7]

In 1983, the United States clashed with both the Bahamas and Canada over an incident involving the Canadian-owned Bank of Nova Scotia. United States authorities had long contended that bank secrecy was being used by United States tax evaders and drug smugglers to launder billions of dollars through Caribbean tax havens like the Bahamas. In the particular case involving the Bank of Nova Scotia, the bank refused to compromise the confidentiality of its customer. In August 1983, the Canadian bank was forced to give a Florida grand jury bank records belonging to a client of its Nassau office after being threatened with a $50,000-a-day fine imposed on the bank's Florida branch.[8] The Pindling government condemned this action as an infringement of Bahamian sovereignty and contrary to international law.

The Bahamas function as an important transshipment point and laundering center for drug money. As early as 1974, the government was aware that narcotics smuggling was developing into a problem. At the time, drug smuggling was not a major business. This changed, however, in the late 1970s. As the *Report of the Bahamas Commission of Inquiry* noted: "The degree of violence was increasing and the foreigners were often armed with the most sophisticated weapons and had up-to-date systems of communication."[9]

The 700 islands of the archipelago were convenient stopping points for *narcotraficantes*, such as Carlos Lehder, who were flying from South America. While the South Americans traded in cocaine and hashish, boats from Jamaica arrived in Bahamian waters, carrying marijuana. Difficult to patrol for government authorities, many islands came to offer refueling services and protection for traffickers. In March 1979, Bahamian police officials identified these islands as The Exumas, Andros, Grand Bahama, Bimini, Abaco, Berry Islands, Cat Island, Crooked Island and Acklins, Ragged Island and Cays.[10] There was a lesser degree of smuggling on Mayaguana, Eleuthera, Long Island, San Salvador, and Inagua.

Bimini, in particular, became a major smuggling point. A Bahamian government report noted: "Because of the very large sums of money involved, it is clear that many officials in Bimini succumbed to corruption and many of local inhabitants took an active part in the transshipment of the drugs."[11]

In the islands, drugs are transferred from long-distance freighters to fast boats and from air cargo aircraft to light airplanes for the final run to Florida or other Gulf states. Official reaction to these developments in the 1970s was slow because drugs were in transit to North America (and therefore was a United States problem), and the transshipment of drugs brought a considerable inflow of capital which helped keep the economy moving forward. This inflow of capital was monitored, in part, by the Governor of the Central Bank of the Bahamas. From 1977 to 1983 the amount of United States dollars transferred from the only bank in Bimini to the Central Bank or deposited in the United States on behalf of the Central Bank were as follows:

| | |
|---|---|
| 1977 | $544,360 |
| 1978 | $1,383,750 |
| 1979 | $3,319,685 |
| 1980 | $5,920,220 |
| 1981 | $3,765,500 |
| 1982 | $4,147,800 |
| 1983 | $12,292,200[12] |

Considering that Bimini has 2,000 inhabitants and the legal economy was based on tourism, it was doubtful that the inflow of money came from licit activities or that wealthy relatives were sending money. The one answer was drugs. The proceeds from the cocaine trade have been reckoned to account for about one-tenth of the country's GDP.[13] For those Bahamians involved, the drug trade was highly lucrative. This situation, however, complicated relations with the United States, the major destination of drugs sent through the Bahamas.

In the early 1980s, growing concern with the drug trade in North America targeted the Bahamas as a problem area. In September 1983, an NBC report alleged that Prime Minister Lyden Pindling and other government officials were receiving $100,000 a month to protect a drug distribution operation run from the islands by fugitive United States businessman Robert Vesco. This created a degree of friction between the Bahamas and the United States and forced Pindling to announce the formation of a blue ribbon Royal Commission to investigate the allegations of bribery and put to rest "unfounded and baseless charges of corruption in the Bahamas."[14]

While the Commission was being formed another incident further marred relations with the United States and cast greater doubt on the Prime Minister's stature. Samuel Leroy Miller, Chairman of the National Progressive Committee, and John Jonathan Rolle, a senior Bahamian immigration officer, were arrested leaving a "sting" operation with $88,000 in cash. The meeting had been with DEA agents, posing as cocaine smugglers, and the money was part of a payment that was eventually supposed to total $300,000. In return for this sum, the two promised protection.

The incident was particularly embarrassing for the Pindling government because of the involvement of a state official as well as a valued political ally of the Prime Minister. Miller, a former restaurant and disco proprietor known as Daddy-O, was an outspoken critic of the DEA's antinarcotics operations in the Bahamas.[15] Only three weeks prior to his arrest, Miller had publicly denounced United States involvement in the investigation of smuggling on Norman's Cay, a remote island allegedly used as a staging base by the Colombian *narcotraficante* Carlos Lehder. In an interview with the *Nassau Guardian*, Miller charged that the Norman's Cay scandal was due to a conspiracy by the press, the DEA, and political opponents of the Prime Minister. At the time, Miller stated: "Many professional Bahamians may find themselves being besmirched by these evil forces in times to come and few of them may be vindicated."[16]

The formation of the Royal Commission came at a politically charged time with both external and domestic charges of corruption. One of the most disturbing aspects of the drug trade in the Bahamas was how it appeared to penetrate the upper levels of government, all the way to the office of Prime Minister Lyndon Pindling. The commission was officially established to investigate "the illegal use of the Bahamas for the transshipment of dangerous drugs destined for the United States."[17] [Allegations of corruption made before it linked some of Pindling's closest friends to drug payoffs, money laundering and influence peddling.][18] Moreover, there were charges that the Prime Minister was linked to Robert Vesco and revelations that he had received millions of dollars in undisclosed loans, gifts, and contributions from foreign businessmen. Although Pindling denied these charges and the commission cleared him, it was noted that his bank accounts reflected deposits of $3.5 million in excess of his salary between 1977 and 1983. The Commission of Inquiry also noted that a number of Friendly Island Commissioners, the representatives of the central government on nearly all the Bahamian Islands:

claimed they either had no direct knowledge of drug trafficking or never received any complaints regarding such activity. . . . We find that to be quite remarkable and we do not believe that they were being candid with us...they could not help but know what was going on in relation to drug trafficking. We have concluded that there must have been a degree of acquiescence on their part....[19]

As to the accusations that Lehder used Norman's Cay, the Commission charged that the *narcotraficante* used that island from 1978 to 1982 as a transshipment base for cocaine. Furthermore, it was charged that local law enforcement figures were paid "substantial bribes." The Commission noted: "Based on the evidence of many witnesses it is clear that the government and senior law enforcement officers were well aware of the fact that drugs were being smuggled through the Bahamas to the United States of America in very significant amounts and that some percentage of the drugs was remaining in the Bahamas and being used by Bahamians."[20]

The charges of corruption and the public debate that followed were not enough to topple Pindling from office. Although five ministers either resigned or were sacked as a result of the probe, the Prime Minister managed to maintain the support of most members of the ruling Progressive Liberal Party (PLP) which had a comfortable majority in the House of Assembly. The PLP had thirty-two of forty-three seats while the opposition Free National Movement had eleven. Even though the debate continued through 1985 and 1986 about corruption in the ruling party, the opposition was unable to capture power in the 1987 elections. This was despite further allegations about government corruption. One case of this was told by "Mickey" Tolliver, a United States pilot. According to Tolliver, one flight he made began in Haiti in July 1986. There he picked up a DC-3 loaded with weapons and ammunition, which was flown to Costa Rica. From Costa Rica he flew to Colombia where he picked up 4,000 pounds of pot and 400–500 kilos of cocaine. His next stop was the Bahamas, where he watched Bahamian police unload the cargo.[21]

Pindling survived politically because under his stewardship of more than eighteen years in office, the Bahamas enjoyed political stability and underwent strong economic growth, especially in the 1980s. Furthermore, United States efforts to "unseat" him stirred up local nationalism. As one Bahamian commented: "How dare the United States tell us what to do with our politics! We are an independent country."[22]

In the 1980s, when the drug trade moved into the islands, the Bahamian economy outperformed practically all other Caribbean countries. Even during the recession in 1981 and 1982, economic growth continued at a pace of 1 percent. In 1983, the country began to pull out of the recession and by 1984 and 1985, GDP expansion was at 3 percent and better. With the exception of 1982, the construction sector was hardly impacted by the recession, growing by 6.3 percent and 6.5 percent in 1984 and 1985 respectively.[23] Though difficult to prove, it is likely that much of the activity in the construction sector was drug-related. A Bahamian government report commented on this trend in Bimini: "Another sign of the sudden increase in the availability of money was the rapid increase in the construction of new buildings by people whose regular source of income had not changed in any way."[24] The drug trade, therefore, helped maintain the economy's expansion and despite a growing internal outcry over corruption, Pindling maintained a majority of the population's political support. Apart from economic reasons, the ruling party remained in office because of the nationalistic backlash to United States pressure vis-à-vis Pindling.

The airing of the debate on the illicit drug trade did have a positive effect in terms of a stronger stance on the part of the government. In March 1985, Operation "Blue Lightning" was launched. Thirty islands were blockaded by United States Coast Guard and Customs, while raids were conducted by Bahamian police and soldiers. Operation Blue Lightning ushered in a brief period of U.S.-Bahamian cooperation in the war on drugs. The raids resulted in the capture of 6,500 pounds of cocaine and 17 tons of marijuana worth $1 million as well as a number of boats and planes.

There has also been a downside to the massive influx of narcotics in the Bahamas. Drug addiction and drug-related crimes have increased as well as prostitution. When the drug trade first developed in the Bahamas few perceived that it would become a domestic problem. By the mid–1980s, medical experts in the Bahamas noted that the amount of cocaine freebasing exceeded anything outside of Colombia.[25] Dr. David Allen, a Bahamian psychiatrist and one of the most important forces behind the need to educate his countrymen to the dangers of cocaine, blamed freebasing for the unprecedented level of violent crime in the country. These crimes included twenty-four shootings in the first half of 1985 (with three fatalities), robberies, and a few rapes. Kelly noted: "more than 11,000 major crimes were reported last year (1985). Nassau, with less than 160,000 population accounted for 70 percent of the total."[26] In many respects, an entire new subclass of drug addicts has been created that lives on the periphery of society and is locked into the drug trade. Moreover, the drug trade has also become the leading (or only) source of income for some of the islands. By the late 1980s, the Bahamas had gradually begun to come to grips with the offshoots of the drug trade— drug addiction, suicides, loss of family income, collapse of the family structure, child abuse, and a rise of violent crime.

One of the most telling comments about the Bahamas' internal addiction problem was stated by Dr. Sandra Dean Patterson: "Breaking the grip that cocaine has on the Bahamas will be impossible unless and until Bahamians decide what their mores are in relation to drugs and what their values are in relation to success."[27] Considering the corruption in the Pindling government, its re-election and the ongoing demand for drugs in the United States, it is doubtful that the Bahamian connection will end in the near future. Relations with the United States in regard to narcotics are also likely to be characterized by ongoing tensions. As one high-ranking DEA agent confided: "In the Bahamas it was very strange. Everytime we pegged a trafficker and wanted to go after him we got a different reaction. On one hand, if the trafficker wasn't linked to Pindling or his chums, the Bahamians responded in a prompt fashion. But if the trafficker was linked to Pindling and company, the keeper of arms couldn't find the keys for the armory to dispense weapons, or he was real slow."[28]

In April 1987, United States Senate hearings were highly critical of the Bahamas and there was an effort to halt United States aid. The Bahamian response was to deny a United States extradition request then pending against Nassau lawyer Nigel Bowe, a Pindling confidant.[29] The United States–Bahamian relationship was further soured in 1987 by revelations that the Miami police in 1984 had planned a "sting" operation that was canceled at the last minute by the State Department, though there were claims that there was sufficient evidence to arrest and try Pindling. One of the high points of the United States–Bahamian tussle was the revoking of the United States ambassador's special parking place in the Bahamas.

In the late 1980s, there is a growing recognition that the drug trade and consumption are problems for the Bahamas. The public airing of the country's dirty laundry has also helped push part of society to act on the problems. Despite certain improvements in enforcement, the scope of the trade and the power of the traffickers remains substantial and, in certain respects, beyond the ability of the government and, more importantly, beyond the leadership elite's political will to find a solution.

## MORE THAN SHIPS GO THROUGH THE PANAMA CANAL

Panama has been called the "crossroads of the world." This title has been given because of the Panama Canal which serves as a conduit between North and South America. As a World Bank report noted: "It is endowed with a geographic location at the crossroads of world trade, a sophisticated, export-oriented commercial sector, an open, well developed financial system, a relatively well trained and frequently bilingual labor force, good communications and an adequate international transport infrastructure."[30] Panama has also benefitted from its geographical position because of its usefulness in the Latin American drug trade, providing services in the laundering of "hot money" and in the transshipping of South American cocaine into the United States. In 1986, Panama was a haven for more than 120 banks; some $600 million in drugs were reported to have passed through the country annually.[31] Panama has refused the United States government access to the bank records and the country's military strongman, General Manual Noriega, has been called "the biggest drug trafficker in the western hemisphere."[32]

Though the drug trade is a relatively new phenomenon in Panama, smuggling is deep-rooted in the country's history. More recently, Panama was a smuggling conduit for weapons from Cuba and South America used in the Sandinista overthrow of the Somoza dynasty in Nicaragua.[33] Panamian strongman General Omar Torrijos had an interest in making certain that Somoza fell from power; hence, he had a major hand in smuggling in the region. That smuggling was not limited to guns and household appliances. Torrijos had ties to one of the "grand old men" of the drug trade, Eduardo Tascón. Tascón was involved in exchanging cocaine for guns in Miami and shipping the guns via couriers to Panama, where a small fleet of aircraft flew them to Tulúa, Colombia. From that point, the weapons were packed into taxis owned by a Tascon-controlled company, and driven to the Ecuadorean border for distribution to guerrilla groups throughout South America. Tascón's connections and the access he provided Torrijos to both guns and drugs appealed to the general. For his own part, Torrijos allegedly received a Paso Fino horse as a gift from Colombian *narcotraficante* Ocampo, to whom he granted "free access to Panama for his aircraft and vessels."[34] Furthermore, the general's brother, Hugo, was the owner of Aerolineas Medellín, "whose nickname, Air Coke, has nothing to do with complimentary beverages."[35]

Torrijos also maintained a working relationship with Cuba, which he used at times as leverage with the United States, especially in negotiations about the Panama Canal. When Torrijos died in a mysterious plane crash in July 1981, he was eventually followed as the head of the military by General Noriega. While Torrijos was a populist figure and held strong nationalistic views, Noriega in 1983 appeared to have a greater interest in maintaining control of the nation's political system as well as enriching himself.

Noriega's rise to power in 1983 was hardly democratic. Since 1968 when the National Guard ousted democratically elected Arnulfo Arias Madrid, power was in the hands of General Torrijos. With the General's death in 1981, power passed to General Rubén Dario Paredes. Paredes, however, was eventually forced out by Noriega who had been number three under Torrijos and responsible for intelligence operations. Both military men after Torrijos ruled the country through a succession of civilian presidents—Aristides Royo, Ricardo de la Espriella, and Jorge

Illueca. For various reasons, these men fell from grace through constitutional coups engineered by the PDF. However, there does appear to
have been a difference between Paredes and Noriega. The former had
begun to dismantle many of the trappings of the Torrijos state and move
toward a more open and pluralistic polity. It is probable that such a
move would have jeopardized the more "shady side" of the PDF's operations and diminished Noriega's influence. The reorganization in 1983
that was responsible for the National Guard becoming the PDF was
pushed by Noriega and clearly enhanced the military's power, especially
as it gained control of customs.

General Noriega was born in 1934 and was an illegitimate child. His
mother put him in a foster home at the age of five. As a teen he won a
scholarship to a military college in Peru and upon graduation he entered
the National Guard as a junior officer posted to Colón Province. He was
transferred after an incident in which he allegedly raped a prostitute.[36]
The officer who helped protect Noriega and who had him transferred
was Torrijos. Noriega's new post was Chiriquí Province, where once
again, there was an alleged rape of a 13-year-old girl. Torrijos once again
intervened, protecting the young officer from legal charges. Torrijos'
loyalty to Noriega was paid in kind when the younger officer helped
quell a coup attempt against his mentor. Noriega was clearly rewarded
as he was soon promoted to the rank of lieutenant colonel and head of
military intelligence. Under military intelligence's jurisdiction were criminal investigations, customs, and immigration. This gave him considerable authority under Torrijos and served as a powerful springboard
into the political arena.

Noriega was careful in consolidating his base of support and since
1983 in containing the opposition. Even before he was the National
Guard's commandant, he was an important force in the clampdown on
*La Prensa*, the major opposition newspaper when it made attacks on
senior officials in the government for drug trafficking and corruption.[37]
When President Illueca challenged Noriega on Panama's involvement
in the Central America Defense Council (Condeca), Noriega had the
country's National Assembly appoint his brother Carlos Noriega Hur-
tado as the president's adviser.[38] Illueca was finally shunted aside when
Noriega decided to support Barletta as a presidential candidate. Barletta's
"narrow" (many have claimed fraudulent) victory over Arias in 1984
was also pushed through by Noriega and the PDF. They wanted opposition leader Arias defeated because he had said he would bring corrupt officers to trial, take away the PDF's customs and immigration
functions, and attack drug trafficking in Panama.[39]

Under Noriega, Panama's involvement in the drug trade increased
considerably. According to Mills, Noriega "has ties to and income from
various traffickers in drugs, arms, and other contraband, as well as

fugitives."[40] Moreover, the Panama Defense Forces, as the National Guard was called after a reorganization in 1983, "provides warehousing for narcotics on their way north, assures the release, for bribes received, of drug traffickers arrested, guarantees the nonarrest of offenders wanted elsewhere who have paid a kind of local safe conduct fee, supervises the air transport of gold, arms, and spies bound to and from North America, Cuba and Central America."[41]

Panama's military leadership ruled the country behind the scenes in the early 1980s, with Noriega throwing his power behind the presidential bid of Nicolas Arditas Barletta in 1984. Though there was considerable discussion about the election being rigged, many were willing to overlook the situation as Barletta appeared to be one of the first civilians to run the country in several years. This enthusiasm, however, died when the new president attempted to implement austerity programs. Moreover, his relations with the National Guard were not good due to the president's independent stance on certain issues. In September 1985, Barletta was forced to resign. This came two weeks after the headless body of Dr. Hugo Spadafora was discovered just over the Panamanian border in Costa Rica.

Spadafora was a former deputy minister of health in the Torrijo's government who had become involved with African revolutionaries, the Sandinistas in Nicaragua, and finally the anti-Sandinista rebels.[42] Since the death of Torrijos, Spadafora had become disenchanted with Noriega and accusations were made that the general was linked to the drug trade. His death therefore became a major event. Demands for an investigation, the fact that witnesses had observed Spadafora with Panamanian police before his death, and outside pressure caused Barletta to announce that the matter would be carefully examined. The president's intention to conduct a meaningful investigation, however, proved to be his undoing as Noriega quickly forced him to resign. Vice President Eric Arturo DelValle then became the fourth president in five years.

After a brief lull in which the issue began to fade from the public's consciousness, Noriega's position as the strongman behind the scenes was threatened anew. This time the challenge came from within the Defense Forces. The Panamanian military's former second in command, Colonel Roberto Diaz Herrera, repeated accusations that Noriega was involved in drug smuggling, the rigging of elections and the murder of political opponents. The former deputy even accused the general of masterminding the 1981 airplane crash of Torrijos. It was also brought into the open that the government had allowed the Colombian drug summit to take place in 1984 in Panama. These allegations quickly became the focus of public attention and prompted thirty-seven civic groups led by Panama's Chamber of Commerce to campaign for Noriega's ouster.[43]

Noriega responded to the situation by accusing his former deputy of treason and conspiracy and had troops seize the Díaz home. Widespread political unrest developed, including demonstrations and riots spearheaded by a middle class that wanted Noriega out of power. Though Noriega was able to ride out the unrest, relations with the United States quickly soured.

Earlier, the United States had trepidation about Noriega's becoming leader of the Defense Forces and the United States government was aware of his ties to the drug trade. The problem then arose as to to how the United States government could deal in good faith with the leader of another country who was involved in the drug trade. This was indeed a perplexing question often raised in the mid and late 1980s and the dilemma was worsened by information apparently provided to the DEA by Spadafora in Costa Rica a month before his death.[44] Jesse Helms, one of the strongest opponents to the Panama Canal Treaties, had few reservations about revealing what was known about Noriega. As the senator stated on the NBC news program "Meet the Press": "there's no question about Mr. Noriega being the biggest . . . head of the biggest drug trafficking operation in the Western Hemisphere."[45] At a conference held at the Johns Hopkins University School of Advanced International Studies later in 1986, many of these same accusations were discussed by former United States Ambassador to Panama (1978–82), Ambler Moss, Roberto Eisenmann, editor at *La Prensa*, Norman Bailey (formerly in the Reagan administration), Steven Ropp, and Ricardo Arias Calderon, President of the Christain Democratic Party in Panama. Most of the participants agreed to the probability of linkages between Noriega and the drug trade. Roberto Eisenmann was probably the most damning in his description of the Noriega-dominated government as "an autocratic military kleptocracy with an ever-shrinking democratic fig leaf."

Bailey's insights were the most informative about the inner workings of the Panamanian government. He noted that linkages to the drug trade could not be discussed without some reference to money-laundering. Bailey asserted that Panama was a major center of drug trafficking and the Panama Defense Force was involved in the trade of both drugs and weapons. Consequently, the entire political structure is involved to varying degrees because the trade brings in large amounts of capital. By one estimate, Panama had $1–1.5 billion circulate through it to the Federal Reserve. This is because Panama uses the US dollar as its currency and must circulate the money back to the United States. Bailey was careful to emphasize that it was not Panama's money as the country was broke and had an external debt of $3.5 billion. As for Spadafora's death, Bailey asserted that he was probably killed by the military on the request of Peruvian *narcotraficantes*. Barletta sought to investigate and was ousted. This led Bailey to comment that as far as he was concerned, the government was "a military dictatorship with a democratic facade, not even a fig leaf."

Many in the United States and Panama found abhorrent the possibility that Noriega was involved in the drug trade. Moreover, other claims that he was spying for Cuba and involved in gun smuggling in Central America did not strengthen his case with either the Liberals or the Conservatives. The movement in the United States was to make public, through hearings on Capitol Hill and elsewhere, the corruption in Panama's armed forces. The other major issue included the lack of democratization.

The United States-Panamanian relationship hit a low point in August 1987 when Washington suspended aid to Panama. In November 1987, tougher measures were taken as the Senate Foreign Relations Committee voted to cut off all but humanitarian aid to Panama until civilian rule was restored. This action also included an embargo on sugar imports from Panama. Despite these external efforts to pressure Noriega to depart and growing domestic opposition, he remained in power. His response to United States "meddling" was to seek closer relations with the Soviet Union and Libya while maintaining pressure on the opposition at home through censorship, intimidation, and coercion.

In 1988, Noriega faced another set of challenges to his hold over the country. Two former regime insiders, José I. Blandón, the Panamanian consul general in New York, and General Paredes publicly acknowledged that Noriega and other top PDF leaders were involved in drug trafficking, corruption, and murder. On February 4, Paredes surprised the country with a radio broadcast in which he accused Noriega of ordering the death of his son, Ruben Paredes, Jr. The younger Paredes was discovered dead, along with a former pilot of General Noriega's, in Medellín, Colombia in 1986 in what diplomatic and intelligence sources described as a drug-related slaying.[46] General Paredes stated that Noriega and a handful of senior officers had corrupted the armed forces by involving them in large-scale drug trafficking and money laundering. After calling on the armed forces to cleanse itself of Noriega and his associates, General Paredes went into hiding.

Blandón's defection was probably more damaging than General Paredes' radio broadcast. Blandón had been a top civilian adviser to Noriega, heading counterintelligence and being a high-ranking official in the government-allied Democratic Revolutionary Party. More than others, Blandón had very good insight into the internal dynamics of the Noriega regime, especially in terms of drug and arms smuggling, corruption, and money laundering. Testifying before the United States government, he linked Noriega to Spadafora's death and revealed that a major diplomatic effort had already been made to ease the strongman from power. Noriega, however, had refused to leave.

The United States government's effort to indict Noriega continued to gather steam with the testimony of a convicted drug smuggler, Steven Kalish. The witness related how he had delivered a briefcase with $300,000 in cash to the general's office in Panama, which was to pay for protection of his activities in that country. Kalish was a key member of a drug ring that arranged the importation of more than 500,000 pounds of marijuana and 3,000 pounds of cocaine into the United States between June 1982 and October 1985.[47] His allegations, according to Senator William V. Roth, Jr., "describe General Noriega as not just aware but as a central agent in drug trafficking and money laundering in Panama."[48]

Other allegations have linked Noriega with both the CIA and Cuban intelligence agencies. Reputedly, Noriega had close ties to the late CIA director, William J. Casey. The relationship with the CIA was reported to have cooled when Casey died. It is highly likely that Noriega played the United States and Cuba off against each other, while receiving financial reimbursement from both for his services. In addition, it has been alleged that the slow pace of bank reform in terms of secrecy laws as requested by the United States government was consistently refused as changes would make it difficult to launder money.

Noriega has consistently denied all charges against him. His response is that the United States is seeking to destabilize Panama so that it can declare the Panama Treaty not binding. He has also sought to generate a number of allegations against the United States government. The most serious was that Admiral Poindexter asked the PDF in a meeting in Panama on December 17, 1985, to invade Nicaragua. This allegation was made on "60 Minutes" aired on February 7, 1988. While Washington denied this, Noriega has also placed the ongoing United States military presence in Panama under pressure, suggesting that they should leave. Instead, the following months witnessed a United States troop build up in Panama, increased tensions between the two governments, and Noriega's crushing of a coup attempt. Noriega was also able to gain some financial support from Cuba, Libya, and some Latin American nations.

General Noriega represents one of the major problems in dealing with the drug trade. In attacking someone like Noriega there is a danger that political "dirt" can be aired that will have embarrassing consequences for branches of the United States government. Embarrassing questions can include: if the United States government knew that Noriega was a major trafficker, why was he on the CIA payroll? Although there are pros and cons in terms of value as an intelligence source, should these issues be debated in public? How does one decide that the source has outlived its usefulness and become more of a liability than an asset? There will be no attempt to answer these questions here, but it is important to consider them in the context of events that unfolded in Panama in 1987 and 1988, and the linkages to the Latin American drug trade.

## THE TALE OF THE CHIEF MINISTER: THE TURKS AND CAICOS ISLANDS

The capital of the British Dependent Territory of the Turks and Caicos Islands is Grand Turk. Its main thoroughfare, Front Street, has fewer than 100 houses, most of which do not exceed two stories. Most of the government's facilities, including the local prison and library, are within five minutes walk of or just off Front Street. In many respects, the capital is a somnolent small town, administrating an archipelago of some forty-two islands and cays, of which only six are inhabited. The Turks and Caicos Islands, therefore, do not appear to be the location of a drama involving the United States and British governments, international banking, a French Canadian businessman, and the Latin American drug trade. Yet, that is precisely what happened when the Chief Minister of the self-governoring British dependency, Norman Saunders, was arrested in Miami with two other senior officials on drug-related charges in March 1985.

The Turks and Caicos Islands, possibly one of the first places that Columbus touched land in 1492, have a history of sailors, slaves, and buccaneers. The first permanent European settlements occurred in the seventeenth century and the islands were used for salt raking and a brief experiment in the plantation cultivation of cotton. The islands advanced through the centuries as part of the British Empire, administered first from the Bahamas and later from Jamaica. When Jamaica became independent in 1962, the archipelago assumed special status as a crown colony. When that nation became independent the Turks and Caicos became a self-governing dependency of the United Kingdom. Its population in the 1980s is around 8,500 and the backbone of the legal economy is a mixture of salt, tourism, offshore banking, and aragonite.

The Turks and Caicos have another economic dimension—the Latin American drug trade. This is not to say that all the people in the Turks and Caicos are involved in the trade. Rather a small, but active minority is, which has important repercussions for the rest of the nation, especially as one of the principals was the territory's elected chief minister. Amelia Smithers noted: "Grand Turk, the capital island, is a sleepy little place where living standards for the majority are still well below those of other UK dependent territories, where using bad language or drinking alcohol in public can land you in the local magistrate's court and where donkeys meander through the dusty streets at rush-hour; a far cry from the sets of Miami Vice."[49]

Despite the relatively sleepy nature of the place, there is the nefarious dimension. The Turks and Caicos have a "convenient" location to Florida and have a tradition of smuggling. During the prohibition period, boot-leggers ran rum into the United States. The many islands and cays made enforcement difficult and, considering the lack of dynamic economic development in other sectors, smuggling, either of rum or cocaine, has had an ongoing appeal as a means of livelihood. It has meant profits for a few in a relatively short period of time and a "trickling down" of the hot money to the other sectors of the economy.

The most recent wave of smuggling wealth came to an end (tempo-rary?) in March 1985 when 41-year-old Chief Minister Saunders, Minister of Commerce and Development Stafford Missick and another member of the ruling Progressive National Party (PNP), and a French Canadian businessman from the Bahamas, Andre Fournier, were arrested in Miami on drug-related charges. This concluded a three-month, United States Drug Enforcement Agency investigation that was conducted with the cooperation of the Turks and Caicos police and the British government. The charges levelled against the group were conspiracy to import nar-cotics into the United States, conspiracy to violate the United States Travel Act, and conducting interstate and foreign travel in aid of rack-eteering enterprises.[50]

The arrests were only the end of what had been a long effort. The Turks and Caicos position as a factor in the smuggling and criminal world has been longstanding, dating back to the 1920s with rum running. In the 1970s, when the smuggling of cocaine and marijuana became an important enterprise, it is possible that other members of the govern-ment were involved in the transit business (i.e., pitstop activities). In 1972, Saunders took control of an aviation fuel company on his home island of South Caicos. Saunders became Chief Minister in 1980 when the island's leading politician, "Jags" McCartney died in a mysterious explosion of an aircraft. Allegedly, the aircraft had a number of under-world figures in it.[51] In the early 1980s, as the United States government sought to take action against the inflow of illegal drugs, the Turks and Ciacos came under suspicion. The United Kingdom at one point sent a special police officer, followed by the initiation of the DEA investigation. This investigation proved largely ineffective, yet produced certain in-sights about the principals.

The DEA proceeded to set up a sting. Agents posed as organizers of a cocaine and marijuana smuggling operation. According to a DEA state-ment, Saunders was alleged to have received $30,000 to ensure safe refueling at South Caicos Island on their journey from Colombia to the United States. During the trial, the prosecution showed a video tape, filmed prior of the arrests, in which Saunders was shown receiving $20,000 from a DEA undercover agent.[52] All three men were convicted in July 1985, and faced sentences of up to thirty years imprisonment.

Saunders, however, was acquitted on the more serious charge of conspiring to import cocaine into the United States.

The March 1985 incident sparked a political crisis in the Turks and Caicos Islands. Saunders was the self-governing territory's chief minister and his two companions were members of the ruling party in the legislature. With Saunders in prison in the United States, the government drifted. The solution was to have a vote of confidence, which, if passed, would permit new elections to be held. The situation was complicated by the fact that the PNP controlled eight of eleven seats. Even without the three missing members of the legislative council, the PNP maintained a 5 to 3 majority. Moreover, if a vote was to be arranged, how would it be handled with three voters sitting in jail in the United States?

The solution was the election of a new chief executive by the legislative council. Former Public Works and Utilities Minister Nathaniel "Bops" Francis was elected. The 72-year-old Francis, however, failed to bring stability to the islands. A number of ruling PNP leaders and members of the opposition were also involved in a series of scandals that included the burning down of one of Grand Turks most historic buildings Bascombe House, incitements of violence through the region, evidence of corrupt practices in the public works department in the award of contracts, the demanding of money from successful contractors, and improper ministerial pressure in the employment and dismissal of staff.[53]

The British reaction to the seeming unraveling of the government in the Turks and Caicos, which originally stemmed from Saunders' arrest, was to conduct an official inquiry into arson, corruption, and related matters; with the evidence from that, to amend the colony's constitution in July 1986. Chief Minister Francis was forced to resign and political authority returned to the British governor, Christopher Turner, who was assisted by four local advisers. The local advisers were all former members of the Legislative Council and had good reputations.

The reaction of the population to the chain of events was one of shock and betrayal. Amelia Smithers noted: "The nature of the sting operation and the fact that it had been carried out with the full knowledge and consent of the Islands' British governor and the British government, was resented by many islanders who thought that the men had been 'set up.' Some thought that the chief minister, who was a popular figure as well as being the national tennis champion, should have been arrested and brought to trial at home."[54]

Despite the disappointment with the situation, the Turks and Caicos Islands remained calm throughout 1986 and 1987. In the months following the arrests, the economy underwent a slump related to the bad publicity the islands received from the incident. However, in 1987, the economy began to improve as the development of other tourist programs moved ahead. Though difficult to prove, it was also likely that the drug trade had quietly been renewed despite the law and order approach of the British governor. Considering the long tradition of smuggling in the Turks and Caicos, it is probable that while a few were caught, the lure has continued. Without alternatives to smuggling and tourism, the drug trade looms as an exciting and lucrative dimension of life.

## OTHER OUTPOSTS AND NEW FRONTIERS

Though Panama, the Turks and Caicos, and the Bahamas are the major transit states, there are other outposts as well as new frontiers. These include the island-states of the Eastern Caribbean, Aruba and the Netherlands Antilles, Barbados, Trinidad and Tobago, the Dominican Republic, Haiti, and Venezuela. There has also been apprehension about drug trafficking in Argentina, Paraguay and Brazil. The strands of the trade permeate the armed forces, enforcement agencies and governments, and have had repercussions on all levels of society. The transit of narcotics has brought money into the societies it has touched, but has also brought domestic consumption, corruption, and addiction.

In the Commonwealth Caribbean there was growing concern about the rise of the drug trade in the late 1980s. Prime Minister John Compton of St. Lucia stated in late 1987: "If the trade continues at the present level the traders will soon be able to control governments."[55] His concern was echoed by Prime Minister A.N.R. Robinson of Trinidad and Tobago: "The power and complexity of the criminal drug network is such that it has penetrated to the very fabric of our societies and threatens to corrupt our most sacred institutions.[56]

Leaders such as Compton and Robinson were apprehensive about the growing use of their island-states as part of drug networks extending from Bolivia and Peru through Guyana and Suriname to North America or from the Colombian-Venezuelan border through the Eastern Caribbean and Hispaniola to North America and Europe. Colombia's drug war and increased United States enforcement measures had caused a search for new routes. Consequently, there was a rising influx of drugs through the Caribbean. This was reflected by the discovery in the Dominican Republic of a ship laden with cocaine (valued at $125 million) from Venezuela to Miami; drug seizures in Puerto Rico; and revelations of the involvement of members of the Duvalier family in trafficking in Haiti. There have also been arrests of high-ranking officials from Suriname and increased incidents of drug smuggling in Guyana.[57]

One of the newest frontiers has been in Venezuela. In the early 1980s, Venezuela was increasingly used as an alternative route. The emergence of the trade in Venezuela occurred, in part, because Colombian traffickers moved operations across the frontier into the neighboring nation.

Another element was the involvement of Trinidadian traffickers. The Trinidadians moved into the Escrecana Delta to refine cocaine as well as in the Pedernates district to establish marijuana plantations.[58] However, the Colombians have been the major outside force in the development of the illicit drug industry.

It was estimated that in 1983 drug trafficking in Venezuela developed into a lucrative $3.2 billion business, accounting for nearly 500,000 consumers.[59] Authorities confiscated 1,200 kilos of cocaine and estimated that, in total, close to 15,000 kilos of the drug were sold in the country. In 1984, the drug trade's tempo increased considerably in this corridor following the crackdown in Colombia. Venezuela, with its long and porous border, was an ideal new launching point of cocaine and marijuana. In addition, Venezuela became a major source for production inputs, like ether and acetone, which came under government controls in Colombia. Alan Riding noted of Venezuela's new role in the trade: "By 1985 it was apparent that the same rivers, roads, and airstrips that were being used to bring the chemicals into Colombia were also being used to smuggle cocaine into Venezuela."[60] Based on cocaine seizures in, or from, Venezuela from 1984–87, one estimate placed between twenty-five and thirty-seven tons of the drug being passed through the country yearly.[61]

Venezuelan authorities did seek to stem the tide. In October 1983, one of the biggest hauls of cocaine—1,200 kilograms—were seized and the involvement of two military men was exposed. One of the officers, a former naval lieutenant, Lizardo Márquez Pérez, escaped to Medellín, Colombia. His copilot, according to the plane's log, was the regional army commander in the region bordering Colombia, General Italo del Valle.[62] In early 1984, an 18,000-hectare marijuana plantation on the slopes of the Sierra de Perija was destroyed. These efforts were made to root out drug use in the armed forces, which was acknowledged to be a problem. Venezuelan authorities also implemented tighter laws against illicit drugs.

Though the Venezuelan government has sought to maintain some control over drug trafficking, it has become a problem in the late 1980s. In 1987 and 1988, there was increased evidence that Venezuela was also becoming a major narcotics producer. This problem has had an impact on relations with Colombia, because many Venezuelans felt that the problem initially came from there. In response, the Venezuelan government sent national guard troops to search and destroy the clandestine marijuana and coca plantations in the Sierra de Perija. In May 1987, a 32-acre drug plantation was discovered and destroyed. In July, a 23-member Venezuelan national guard patrol was attacked by Colombians, leaving eighteen dead soldiers. General Marcial Rojas Aguero, the head of the National Guard's Intelligence division, identified the attackers as "narcoguerrillas of Colombia's *Ejército de Liberación Nacional* (ELN).[63] It was also felt that the attack on the patrol was in retaliation for the destruction of the plantation. The problem of the border continued into 1988 and remains a point of friction between the two countries.

In the mid and late 1980s, the drug trade has overlapped into other regions as well. Bolivian coca paste was sent to neighboring Argentina and Brazil for processing and transshipment. There has also been concern about rising marijuana production in Paraguay. In addition, Central America emerged as a major transshipment point to North American markets.

The "Central American connection" has probably been the most controversial as rumors abound linking both the Sandinistas and *contras* in Nicaragua, the Central Intelligence Agency, officials in the Reagan administration, the Cubans, and various military establishments in Honduras and Guatemala. In an atmosphere thick with allegations and counterallegations and colored by ideological perceptions, it would appear that almost everyone is involved, except the Catholic church.

In Honduras, the transshipment of drugs increased substantially in 1986 and 1987. Attention to trafficking in that Central American nation resulted from an incident involving a Honduran military attache, Army Colonel William Said Speer. In December 1987, the Honduran government recalled the colonel from Colombia after Jorge Luis Ochoa, a member of the Medellín cartel was arrested November 21 in Bogotá while driving Said Speer's sportscar, a 1987 Porsche. Wilson Ring, a journalist, touched the core of the matter: "There was no immediate explanation of how Said Speer, who earns $30,000 a year as an army colonel, came to possess a car estimated to cost more than $100,000 in Colombia."[64]

The Honduran "connection" loomed even larger on April 5, 1988, when Juan Matta Ballesteros, linked to the Camarena murder in Mexico, was arrested in his native Honduras and flown to the Dominican Republic. In the island republic, United States marshals were waiting and took him to the United States. While this was a significant victory for anti-drug forces, the *narcotraficantes* were able to make Matta Ballesteros's arrest a matter of Honduran nationalism. Days later, a large crowd burned down part of the United States embassy in Tegucigalpa. There is a strong possibility that drug money was used to help motivate the crowd.

Along with other incidents in Honduras there have been rumors of drug trafficking in Costa Rica, El Salvador and Guatemala. The unsettled political nature of much of the region and the involvement of a wide range of outside actors, ranging from arms smugglers and *narcotraficantes* and rightwing counter-revolutionaries, has made ideal conditions for the drug trade. Borders are more difficult to patrol, identities are easier to be confused, and clandestine operations take on the air of near-normalcy.

## CONCLUSION

The transportation-laundering nexus is an important part of the Latin American drug trade. Without it, drug traffickers would have considerably more difficulty in evading enforcement measures and laundering their profits. Additionally, narcomoney has had an impact on the economies and societies throughout the Caribbean and Central America, as reflected by events in the Bahamas and Panama. Part of the problem is developmental: the enormous amounts of narcodollars that can be offered to government officials and other members of society are well beyond most legal means of making a living. That amount of capital also has a tremendous impact on employment, legal business generation, and progressive economic growth, including improved living conditions. The other part of the problem is a matter of political will: there is a need for political, social, and economic leaders to stand up to the hydra's head of problems related to the drug trade. Though there are growing segments of governments and citizenry in the Caribbean, Central America and other transit states that are becoming concerned with the situation, firm political leadership remains an essential item—something that has been lacking in Panama under Noriega and in the Bahamas under Pindling. In other cases, it has been firm leadership that has pushed governments into the drug trade as in the cases of Cuba and Nicaragua which are discussed in the next chapter.

## NOTES

1. Quoted in Permanent Subcommittee on Investigations of the Committee on Governmental Affairs, United States Senate, *Crime and Secrecy: The Use of Offshore Banks and Companies* (Washington, D.C.: U.S. Government Printing Office, August 28, 1985, p. 17.

2. Much of the rest of this paragraph is paraphrased from the above source, p. 17. Those nations that are listed as tax havens or that have offshore facilities are Antigua and Barbuda, Austria, Bahamas, Bahrain, Barbados, Belize, Bermuda, British Virgin Islands, Cayman Islands, Costa Rica, Channel Islands, Gibralter, Grenada, Hong Kong, Isle of Man, Liberia, Liechtenstein, Luxembourg, Monaco, Nauru, the Netherlands, the Netherlands Antilles, Panama, Singapore, St. Kitts-Nevis, St. Vincent and the Grenadines, Switzerland, Turk and Caicos Islands, and Vanautu (formerly the New Hebrides in the South Pacific).

3. Yoon S. Park and Jack Zwick, *International Banking in Theory and Practice* (Reading, Mass.: Addison-Wesley Publishing Company, 1985), p. 155.

4. Ibid.

5. For more information on the structure of the Bahamian banking system see Samuel J. Stephens, "Fiancial System of the Bahamas," in Robert C. Effros (editor), *Emerging Financial Centers: Legal and Institutional Framework* (Washington, D.C.: International Monetary Fund, 1982), pp. 5–99.

6. "Bahamas: Still a flourishing offshore centre," *The Latin American Times*, April 29, 1987, p. 29.

7. Ibid.

8. Nicki Kelly, "Bahamas Sets Talks on Secrecy," *Journal of Commerce*, December 22, 1983, p. 6.

9. Bahamas Commission of Inquiry, *Report of the Commission of Inquiry Appointed to Inquire into the Illegal Use of the Bahamas for the Transshipment of Dangerous Drugs Destined for the United States of America, November 1983-December 1984* (Nassau, The Bahamas: The Commission, 1984), p. 8.

10. Ibid.

11. Ibid., p. 10.

12. Ibid., p. 13.

13. "The Caribbean: Open Palms among the Palm Trees," *The Economist*, October 11, 1986, p. 47.

14. Carl Hiaasen, "Bahamas charged with drug payoffs," *Miami Herald*, October 30, 1983, p. 6.

15. Ibid.

16. Ibid.

17. Robert Pear, "Clamor Is Growing in the Bahamas for Premier's Resignation," *The New York Times*, October 22, 1984, p. A6.

18. Nicki Kelly, "Bahamas PM Survives after pledge of respectability," *The Financial Times*, October 30, 1984, p. 4.

19. Bahamas Commission of Inquiry, *Report to the Commission of Inquiry Appointed to Inquire Into the Illegal Use of the Bahamas*, 1984, Note 303, pp. 175–176.

20. Ibid., p. 67.

21. Recounted in Leslie Cockburn, *Out of Control: The Story of the Reagan Administration's Secret War in Nicaragua, the Illegal Arms Pipeline, and the Contra Drug Connection* (New York: Atlantic Monthly Press, 1987), p. 184.

22. Interview with Bahamian citizen in Washington, D.C. in June 1986.

23. Inter-American Development Bank, *Economic and Social Progress in Latin America: 1986 Report* (Washington, D.C.: Inter-American Development Bank, 1986), p. 196.

24. Bahamas Commission of Inquiry, *Report of the Commission of Inquiry Appointed to Inquire Into the Illegal Use of the Bahamas*, p. 14.

25. Nicki Kelly, "Cocaine money breeds trouble in the Bahamas," *The Financial Times*, July 19, 1983, p. 5.

26. Ibid.

27. Ibid.

28. Comments made to author by former DEA agent in interview in 1985.

29. *Latin America Regional Reports Caribbean*, May 14, 1987, pp. 5–6.

30. World Bank, *Panama: Structural Change and Growth Prospects* (Washington, D.C.: The World Bank, 1985), p. xxiv.

31. *The Economist*, October 11, 1986, p. 47.

32. Ibid.

33. Robert Pastor, *Condemned to Repetition* (Princeton: Princeton University Press, 1987), p. 126.

34. James Mills, *The Underground Empire: Where Crime and Governments Embrace* (Garden City, New York: Doubleday & Company, Inc., 1986), p. 883.

35. Ibid.

36. Nancy Cooper, et al., "Drugs, Money and Death," *Newsweek*, February 15, 1988, p. 34.

37. *Latin America Regional Reports Mexico and Central America*, December 2, 1983, p. 8.

38. *Latin America Weekly Report*, May 4, 1984, p. 5.

39. *Latin America Weekly Report*, May 18, 1984, p. 11.

40. James Mills, *The Underground Empire*, p. 1132.

41. Ibid.

42. David Asman, "Another Shakey U.S. Ally," *The Wall Street Journal*, April 3, 1986, p. 26.

43. Stephen Baker, "Turmoil in Panama Has Its Strongman Tottering," *Business Week*, August 3, 1987, p. 42.

44. James LeMoyne, "Panama General Accused in Killing," *The New York Times*, June 20, 1986, p. 15.

45. John Herbers, "Panama General Accused by Helms," *The New York Times*, June 23, 1986, p. 15.

46. Larry Rohter, "Noriega Ordered Colombia Slaying, Predecessor Says," *The New York Times*, February 5, 1988, p. A6.

47. Joe Pichirallo and Bob Woodward, "Drug Figure Linked to Noriega Payoff," *The Washington Post*, January 28, 1988, p. A1.

48. Ibid.

49. Amelia Smithers, "Turks and Caicos Islands," in *The Latin America and Caribbean Review* (Harmondsworth, United Kingdom: World of Information, 1987), p. 209.

50. Robert Graham, "Drugs Scandal Rocks Caribbean Islands," *The Financial Times*, March 5, 1985, p. 5.

51. Ibid.

52. Amelia Smithers, "Turks and Caicos Islands," in *Latin America and Caribbean Review 1986* (Harmondsworth, United Kingdom: World of Information, 1986), p. 212.

53. Ibid.

54. Ibid.

55. Canute James, "Drug smugglers turn to Caribbean island-hopping," *The Financial Times*, November 13, 1987, p. 5.

56. Ibid.

57. Rod Neyist, "Guyana 1988: Drugs and Garbage," *Friends for Jamaica Caribbean Newsletters*, February-March 1988, Vol. 8, No. 1, p. 1.

58. Frank Fonda Taylor, "Does Trinidad Have a Drug Problem," *Caribbean Review* 15, no. 4 (Spring 1987), p. 15.

59. *Latin America Weekly Report*, February 3, 1984, p. 5.

60. Alan Riding, "Cocaine Finds A New Route In Venezuela," *The New York Times*, July 18, 1987, p. A15.

61. Estimate of Vladimir Gessen, member of the Venezuelan Congress who heads the Subcommission to Prevent Improper Use of Drugs; quoted in Riding.

62. *Latin America Weekly Report*, February 10, 1984, p. 8.

63. *Latin America Weekly Report*, July 2, 1987, p. 3.

64. Wilson Ring, "U.S. Looks at Honduras as Drug Transfer Point," *Washington Post*, December 7, 1987, p. A27. Also see Bradley Graham, "Impact of Colombian Traffickers Spreads," *The Washington Post*, February 24, 1988, p. A22.

# 8

# The Cuban and Nicaraguan Connections

## INTRODUCTION

Nowhere has discussion about the Latin American drug trade been more heated than in the cases of Cuba and Nicaragua. Both countries are involved in the transshipment of cocaine and other drugs to North America, much like other nations in the region. The ideological differences between the United States on one hand, and Cuba under Fidel Castro and Nicaragua under the Sandinistas on other hand, has made this an even more sensitive matter. The debate began in 1959 when Castro and the July 26th Movement took power from the corrupt Batista regime and launched the "revolution." Since that period, United States-Cuban relations have usually been hostile. It is not surprising that the Latin American drug trade would, in some fashion, overlap into an already bitter relationship. Cuba is very much involved in the drug trade, functioning as a coordinator in the drugs-for-arms business that links them with both *narcotraficantes* and leftist guerrillas. Since the early 1980s, Nicaragua has also been involved, but to a lesser extent.

The purpose of this chapter is to examine the Cuban and Nicaraguan connections in the Latin American drug trade. These two Marxist countries are important forces behind the drug-insurgency nexus in Latin America. This is not to say that Cuba and Nicaragua are the sole causes for revolutionary activity in the region because that would be a simplistic explanation for a complicated problem. As these two countries are revolutionary states, the natural course for most revolutions is to create other nations in the same image; hence, the need to help similar-minded forces in the region. The drug-insurgency nexus provides one weapon with which the "forces of international imperialism" may be struck, especially as it carries the "struggle" to the United States and makes casualties of its younger generations. Consequently, one of the major reasons for Cuban and Nicaraguan involvement has been ideological. Another important reason is that the drug trade provides hard currency, something that both countries are usually lacking. This is underscored as both countries have had problems with their foreign debt, each having to reschedule at least once. A last possible reason is the most fundamental of all and is something that binds those in North and South America together in the drug trade—greed. Though difficult to prove, it is likely that a degree of corruption does exists in both nations and someone benefits more than others from the trade.

This chapter will not take an in-depth view of the Reagan administration's involvement in Nicaragua and the possible links between members of the United States government and drug and arms traffickers in Central America. As a topic, it has been dealt with elsewhere in much greater length and any discussion in this volume would detract from the main thrust of examining the Latin American drug trade in a holistic fashion.[1]

## CUBA'S INVOLVEMENT IN THE DRUG TRADE

Cuba shares with the Bahamas as one of the best locations from which to smuggle goods into the United States. Located within one hundred miles of Florida, the island-state's government also has an incentive to retaliate against its northern neighbor. Cuban-United States relations have been strained since the Castro revolution in 1959. Part of the problem stemmed from the fact that Fidel Castro and his close associates, such as Raul, his brother, and Ernesto "Ché" Guevera, intentionally moved Cuba into a Marxist-Leninist political system, which was anti-United States and pro-Soviet Union. As the revolution radicalized in the early 1960s, the Cuban government nationalized all United States assets on the island. In response, the United States suspended relations. From that point forward, the relationship worsened with the United States aiding the Bay of Pigs exile attempt to oust the leftist regime in 1961. Other operations included assassination attempts, sabotage, an economic embargo, diplomatic isolation, and bombings of Cuban equipment and personnel overseas. For their part, the Cubans were hardly poor victims, as the new regime sought to export revolution to Central and South America, the Caribbean and Africa. Throughout the 1960s to the present, Cuban and United States foreign policy objectives have usually been marked by mutual suspicion and hostility. Consequently, the idea that Cuba would seek to make use of the drug trade (and narcoterrorism) as a means of striking at the United States and its regional allies has a certain logic.

There are a few other important aspects of Cuba's involvement in the drug trade. Fidel Castro once stated: "We are going to make the people up there [the United States] white, white with cocaine."[2] While Castro's motives for involvement can be explained in terms of his onging campaign against the United States, there is an additional element to be considered in the context of Cuba's ties to the Soviet Union. There is a question of the Soviet maintaining the Cuban economy at a cost of around $4 billion annually. Part of that cost has been in the training and equipping of Cuban intelligence agencies—the General Directorates of Intelligence (DGI), Departmento America (DA), and the General Directorate of State Security (DGSE). Timothy Ashby noted: "Augmentation of the operating budgets of the DGI, DA, and DGSE with narcotics proceeds also benefits Moscow by reducing financial obligations to its Caribbean proxies."[3] The Soviets did not invent arms or drug trafficking, but in the case of Cuba they have found it to be a useful weapon against United States interests.

The first reports of Cuban government involvement in drug trafficking were in the early 1960s, but these were not fully substantiated. In 1983 Francis "Bud" Mullen, then the Acting Administrator of the DEA, stated: "As early as 1963, DEA predecessor agencies received information alleging a government of Cuba in drug trafficking."[4] Considering the difficult economic conditions in Cuba at the time because of the United States embargo, the drug trade would have provided badly needed hard currency that otherwise was not available. At the same time there is evidence that internally, the Castro regime moved to eradicate the use of drugs.[5]

In the 1970s, there were further accounts of Cuban involvement in the drug trade. According to one source, some of Colombia's largest *narcotraficantes* met in Bogota in late 1975 with the Cuban Ambassador Fernándo Revélo Renédo to negotiate the release of ships and crews seized in Cuban waters.[6] What the Colombians got, however, far surpassed expectations. The Cubans offered protection, refueling and repair services in the country's ports in return for payments which were to be used to help leftist groups in Central America and the Caribbean. Moreover, the smugglers who carried drugs north could ferry weapons and supplies for guerrilla forces on their trips south. Of particular importance to Cuba's geopolitical view was Colombia, one of the largest South American nations with a long-standing guerrilla problem. It was also logistically closer than Peru or Bolivia. In the testimony of José Blandón in February 1988, a high-ranking Panamanian official, Castro's strategy for Colombia was: "if you want to have an influence on Colombia's political world, you have to have an influence on the drug trafficking world too."[7] In the late 1970s, the Cubans apparently moved in this direction, developing linkages with the Medellín cartel. Asked how the Cuban leader could justify being part of the cartel's drug operation, Blandón told the Senate Foreign Relations Subcommittee on Terrorism, Narcotics and International Affairs: "Fidel's view of the situation was that the war in Central America waged by the United States made it easier or at least gave him a moral justifiction to do anything against the United States, anything that was necessary."[8]

It was not until the early 1980s that Cuba's role in trafficking was more substantially documented. The arrest and conviction of Colombian *narcotraficante* Jaime Guillot Lara opened a window on Cuban drug operations in the United States and Caribbean Basin. A DEA investigation revealed that Guillot Lara was the owner of a small fleet of ships capable of smuggling tons of marijuana and cocaine. It was documented that he sent into the United States through Cuba a total of 2.5 million pounds of marijuana, 25 million methaqualone tablets, and 80 pounds of cocaine in the years between 1977 and 1981.[9]

According to one Cuban defector, when Colombian boats left their country with drugs they carried the Cuban flag which was used once Cuban waters were reached.[10] This notified Cuban authorities that the ship was friendly. Cuban patrol craft would then come to the mother ships to escort them into a key, Cayo Paredon Grande. Cuban officers then viewed the exchange when ships coming from the United States would arrive to transfer the narcotics from the mother ship into smaller vessels. Those ships were escorted to a limit close to the United States, possibly around the 10-mile limit, where they then take down the Cuban flag and discard it. Another dimension of this trade was the smuggling of United States goods, such as televisions and Batamax machines, into Cuba for officials there.

Guillot Lara's first contact with the Cubans took place in Bogotá in late 1979. Introduced to Cuban embassy personnel by another trafficker, it was suggested to the Colombian that he use Cuba as a transshipment point as government protection would be provided. In July 1980, Guillot Lara met again with the Cubans to discuss the issue in a more serious manner. Shortly thereafter, he began moving his drugs through Cuba where he was charged $10 per pound of marijuana.[11] This gave the Cubans hundreds of thousands of dollars for each load of drugs. Guillot Lara also arranged with Cubans in Panama and Mexico arms deliveries to M–19 in Colombia. There was also supposed to be a future arms shipment sent to an unspecified group in Bolivia.

What did Cuba do with its narcodollars? According to Mullen: DEA learned that Cuba's facilitation of Guillot's smuggling ventures provided hard currecy which Cuba used to support revolutionary activities in Latin America. Cuba was also able to utilize the smuggling expertise and capabilities of Guillot by having him transport and deliver arms which were ultimately destined for the Colombian terrorist group, M–19, led by Guillot's close friend, Jaime Bateman.[12]

Guillot Lara's enterprises, however, were not always successful. In November 1981, one of his ships, the *Karina* was spotted offloading waspons on the Pacific coast of Colombia. Colombian navy patrol boats sank the ship and from the few survivors learned that the weapons were for M–19. Lara Guillot fled to Cuba, where he could expect a safe haven. It had only been a month earlier that Fidel Castro had told Colombian journalists that the fugitive was "a good friend of Cuba." Cuba's "good friend" then traveled to Nicaragua, where he met with Raul Castro, the leading Cuban official directing the drug trade. From Nicaragua, the Colombian went to Mexico City where he was to meet with Cuban embassy officials. However, he was arrested on false documentation charges on November 25, 1981. Requests for extradition from both Colombia and the United States were denied and in September 1982, he was released. From Mexico, Guillot Lara disappeared, possibly to Spain.

In November 1982, the United States District Court indicted Guillot Lara and four other high-ranking Cubans on charges of conspiracy to smuggle drugs. Those Cubans were Rene Rodriguez Cruz, a leading officer of the Cuban intelligence service, Dirección General de Inteligencia (D.G.I.) and a member of the Cuban Communist Party Central Committee; Aldo Santamaria Cuadrado, a vice-admiral of the Cuban navy and a member of the CCP Central Committee; Fernándo Ravélo and Renédo, the former Cuban ambassador to Colombia; and Gonzalo Bassols Suarez, a former minister-counsel of the Cuban embassy in Bogota. United States Attorney Stanley Marcus' testimony of April 30, 1983 argued that the Cubans and Guillot Lara were involved in a conspiracy that stretched from the growers and drug merchants in Colombia to middlemen and exporters to shippers and ship crews, including high-ranking Cuban officials. According to witnesses, like Juan Crump and David Pérez, Cuban officials sought out *narcotraficantes* in Colombia and offered passage through Cuban waters to evade the United States interdiction effort and reprovision for the ships. Crump was a Colombian lawyer and a narcotics trader who had been the go-between for Guillot Lara and the Cuban embassy officials. Pérez was a Cuban-American smuggler, with considerable experience in Cuban waters.

A third witness, Mario Estevez González, was a Cuban agent infiltrated into the United States during the Mariel Boatlift in 1980. According to his testimony, he was given orders to traffic in drugs and send the earnings back to his Cuban control officers. In addition, the Mariel Boatlift had been the cover to infiltrate a large number ("at least 3,000") of

Cuban intelligence officers, "many of whom had been trained specifically to cultivate the drug trade."[13]

It was the evidence of Pérez and Estevez that linked Vice Admiral Santamaría and Rodríquez to the trade. According to the former witness, the two had met a shipment of methaqualones in Cuban waters while heading to the United States. Rodriquez had stated that he was "happy" that Perez was bringing so many drugs into the United States.[14] González, the former agent smuggled into the United States during the Mariel Boatlift, further testified that the Vice Admiral said to the crew of the smuggling boat: "We are going to fill Miami completely with drugs . . . so that more young Americans will die."[15]

While United States charges against Cuba for its involvement in the Latin American drug trade are often portrayed as anti-Cuban propaganda, they are taken more seriously in countries like Colombia. In July 1980 Cuban intelligence officers arranged a unity meeting of representatives of the rival M–19, ELN, and FARC in Panama.[16] The Cuban intention was to create a more effective rebel front. This strategy had been successful in Nicaragua and it is likely that the Cuban government felt a similar approach had a chance in Colombia. In March 1981, Colombia President Julio Turbay Ayala suspended diplomatic relations with Cuba following the capture of several dozen M–19 guerrillas near the Ecuadorian border.[17] The Colombians were upset because the guerrillas were trained and armed in Cuba and returned to Colombia via Panama. The captured guerrillas had also implicated the Cuban Embassy as a M–19 recruitment center. Other incidents linked the Cubans to Colombia's various guerrilla groups, who, in turn, had ties to the *narcotraficantes*. In a sense, the trade in drugs financed the purchase of weapons which were then used to combat government troops or involved in acts of political terrorism. Behind the scenes, working as a coordinator, were the Cubans.

## NICARAGUA AND THE TRADE

Brian Freemantle wrote of Cuba in 1986: "For a impoverished country committed to spreading leftist revolution throughout Latin America, drugs provide the perfect answer."[18] The same could be said of Nicaragua since the Sandinistas (*Frēnte Sandinista de Liberación Nacional* or FSLN) came to power in 1979. While Cuba's role in the drug trade in the 1980s was regarded as an important development, the involvement of Nicaragua in the same role has become a battlefield of opinions between those who favor and those who oppose the Reagan administration's Central American policies. Propaganda from both sides abounds, leaving truth the probable casualty.

CBS news reporter Leslie Cockburn, in a very lopsided account of the

"Secret War in Nicaragua, the Illegal Arms Pipeline, and the Contra Drug Connection," argued that the *contras* were major traffickers and did so with the United States government's blessings.[19] According to Cockburn, the *contras* funded their "war effort" with drug money and were aided in this by the Central Intelligence Agency and Reagan administration officials like Lt. Col. Oliver North. In a sense, Cockburn was discussing the drug-insurgency nexus with the contras fulfilling the role of the guerrillas, aided by the United States in the role of the Cubans, and the Sandinistas in the role of the government of Colombia or Peru.

Another journalist, Brian Barger, supports much of what Cockburn wrote, but in a more balanced fashion, noting that the Colombian *narcotraficantes* "have made comfortable bedfellows cross the political spectrum, from the fascist death squads in Argentina and Colombia to Maoist guerrillas in Peru."[20] It would then not be entirely outrageous to suggest that both sides of the conflict in Nicaragua, the Sandinistas and *contras*, are involved in the drug trade. The primary motivations are revenue raising and personal greed.

Reports of Sandinista interest in drug trafficking began to surface in 1981. It was alleged that the Sandinistas were involved in the trade and sought to make their country a transshipment point. Nicaraguan Interior Ministry defector Alvaro Baldizon documented Sandinista Comandante Tomas Borge's involvement in cocaine trafficking for the purpose of obtaining United States currency to help finance the FSLN's revolutionary and subversive operations.[21] This was reinforced in July 1983 when Rodolfo Palacios Talavera, former First Secretary of the Nicaraguan Embassy in Ottawa was arrested by Canadian police for possession of cocaine valued at $10,000 in United States currency. There were also reports that Borge allowed Colombian traffickers to use Corn Island (off the east coast of Nicaragua) as a transshipment point for northbound drugs.

In another instance, Robert Vesco, now living in Cuba, acted as a middleman for Colombian *narcotraficantes* Carlos Lehder and Pablo Escobar in a deal with Frederico Vaughan, an aide to Nicaraguan Interior Minister Tomas Borge, to import cocaine into the United States.[22] According to Barger, in early 1984 "Sandinista officials allegedly agreed to provide security for smuggling operations through Nicaragua, and to allow the relocation of cocaine-processing labs to remote parts of the country."[23] The result of this interest was documentation of Sandinista involvement in the drug trade. In June 1984, Adler Barriman Seal, a former Ochoa cocaine trafficker working with the DEA, took pictures of Vaughan and Escobar, escorted by Nicaraguans in uniform, helping to load cocaine into his aircraft. Seal had earlier flown from Colombia with a load of cocaine and left it in Nicaragua at an airport near Managua. During another trip in July 1984, Seal taped Vaughan saying that a cocaine processing center was ready for use.[24] Although Seal was later assassinated in the United States, he had proven instrumental in revealing the level of Sandinista involvement.

As in the case of Cuba, the question of motives arises. In July 1979, the Sandinistas came to power after a bitter civil war with the corrupt regime of Anastasio Somoza. During the fighting, considerable damage was done to the country's infrastructure and the new government's ability to meet its international debt obligations, which were a little over $2 billion was greatly hampered. By 1982, the Nicaraguan economy began to slip into a recession. The GDP growth rate that year was $-0.8$ percent, resulting from a reduced level of investment, a decline in exports, and a shortage of essential imports.[25] This situation was reflected in the country's balance of payments that showed a current account deficit of $479 million. The situation worsened throughout the decade as the current account continued to widen, the size of the external debt expanded from $2.5 billion in 1982 to a little over $4.7 billion in 1985, and inflation rose from 24 percent in 1981 to 219.5 percent in 1985.[26] The largest sector of the economy, agriculture, accounting for about 41 percent of the GDP, was "affected by the guerrilla war operations, which forced many farmers to abandon their land and seek refuge in other regions; the difficulty of finding workers to harvest crops, especially in areas of fighting; and problems with the timely supply of some imported inputs and replacement parts."[27] The other sectors of the economy, from manufacturing to mining, also were affected by the impact of the *contra* war effort.

The overriding concern for the Sandinista leadership has been the consolidation of their power base inside the country and, secondly the export of revolution. To achieve both objectives, the Sandinistas moved to quickly develop their armed forces into one of the largest military organizations in Latin America. The development of the armed forces was accomplished with considerable assistance from the Soviet Union and Cuba. In fact, advisers from those countries and other East European nations have been part of the ongoing friction between the Central American nation and the United States.

One of the more important dimensions of Cuban, Soviet, and East German involvement in Nicaragua has been the development of a relatively effective intelligence apparatus. The General Directorate of State Security (DGSE) was staffed in part with Cubans and Soviets and a smaller number of East German and Bulgarian advisers. As one source commented: "The Soviets and their East European allies provide facilities, training and equipment to the DGSE, in addition to operational guidance."[28] Both the Cubans and the Bulgarians are known to be involved in the drug trade—clearly this is one area they could provide some advice to the Nicaraguans.

One offshoot of this has been the emergence of Nicaragua as an important linkage in the drug-insurgency nexus in Latin America. Since its period in the political wilderness in the 1960s and early 1970s, the FSLN has maintained contacts with a number of terrorist organizations and radical states. Many of the leading Sandinistas trained and fought with Palestine Liberation Organization guerrillas; Libya has been a supplier of military equipment, advisers and technical personnel, and assistance has been provided to leftist Salvadorean rebels. The various Central American groups have been provided with safe houses, financial and military assistance, and medical aid. The wider range of FSLN ties was noted in *The Latin American Times*:

The Sandinistas' ties are not limited to groups in Central America, however, for they also have links with groups such as the Montoneros of Argentina, the 19th of April Movement (M–19) of Colombia, the Movement for the Revolutionary Left (MIR) of Chile, the Tupamoros of Uruguay, the Basque Homeland and Liberty (ETA) separatist movement of Spain, the Baader-Meinhoff gang of Germany, and the Red Brigades of Italy. (In February 1985, Italian Prime Minister Bettino Craxi complained in a public statement before the Italian Parliament that Nicaragua had become a safehaven for fugitive Italian terrorists.) Some of these groups have been implicated in terrorist attacks against the Sandinistas' opponents carried out in third countries.[29]

Considering the poor condition of the economy, the involvement in the terrorist-revolutionary network in Latin America and elsewhere, close ties to a number of countries involved in narcotics transshipment (like Bulgaria and Cuba), and the ongoing conflict with the *contras*, the attraction of earning sizeable amounts of foreign currency through the drug trade has been high and, in a relatively warped sense, logical. The conclusion, drawn through evidence such as that provided by Seal and defectors, is that the FSLN is indeed involved in the trade. As one report noted: "foreign currency needed to help sustain operations is obtained in part through drug transactions."[30]

## CONCLUSION

The drug trade has affected almost all governments in the Western Hemisphere and those countries professing revolutionary doctrines have not been immune. In fact, because of their revolutionary doctrine, the drug trade has become part of the war against the "forces of world imperialism." Cuba and Nicaragua clearly are involved in the drug-insurgency nexus in Latin America, helping coordinate the movement of drugs north into the United States and Canada and the movement of weapons south to guerrilla organizations. To date, there is little evidence of internal consumption of either marijuana or cocaine because those governments oppose pollution of their respective societies. However, the danger of drug use spreading exists despite the high level of societal control. Other Latin and Caribbean countries felt immune to local drug consumption, and in the late 1980s have watched as the problem became their own. Likewise, Cuba and Nicaragua, who have been playing with fire, are risking getting burned.

## NOTES

1. For further reading see Leslie Cockburn, *Out of Control: The Story of the Reagan Administration's Secret War in Nicaragua, the Illegal Arms Pipeline, and the Contra Drug Connection* (New York: The Atlantic Monthly Press, 1987), and Bob Woodward, *Veil: The Secret Wars of the CIA 1981–1987* (New York: Simon and Schuster, 1987).

2. Uri Ra'anan, Robert Pfaltzgraff, Jr., Richard Shultz, Ersnt Halperin and Igor Lukes (editors), *Hydra of Carnage* (Lexington, Mass.: Lexington Books, 1986), p. 330.

3. Timothy Ashby, *The Bear in the Back Yard: Moscow's Caribbean Strategy* (Lexington, Mass.: Lexington Books, 1987), p. 165.

4. "The Cuban Government Involved in Facilitating International Drug Traffic," Transcript from Hearings before the Senate Drug Enforcement Caucus, the Senate Judiciary Subcommittee on Security and Terrorism and the Senate Foreign Relations Subcommittee on Western Hemisphere Affairs, April 30, 1983.

5. Brian Freemantle, *The Fix: Inside the World Drug Trade* (New York: Tom Doherty Associates, Inc., 1986), p. 256.

6. Nathan M. Adams, "Havana's Drug-Smuggling Connection," *Reader's Digest*, July 1982.

7. Bradley Graham, "Impact of Colombian Traffickers Spreads," *The Washington Post*, February 24, 1988, p. A22.

8. Ibid.

9. The Senate Judiciary Subcommittee on Security and Terrorism, "The Cuban Government Involvement," *Transcript*, p. 44.

10. The Cuban American National Foundation, *Castro and the Narcotics Connection* (Washington, D.C.: The Cuban American National Foundation, 1983), pp. 20–21.

11. The Senate Judiciary Subcommittee on Security and Terrorism, "The Cuban Government Involvement," *Transcript*, p. 45.

12. Ibid.

13. Brian Freemantle, *The Fix*, p. 257.

14. The Cuban American National Foundation, *Castro and the Narcotics Connection*, p. 11.

15. President's Commission on Organized Crime, *America's Habit: Drug Abuse, Drug Trafficking, and Organized Crime* (Washington, D.C.: U.S. Government Printing Office, March 1986), p. 135.

16. Robert S. Leiken, *Soviet Strategy in Latin America* (New York: The Washington Papers/Praeger Publishers, 1982), p. 90.

17. Don Bohning, "U.S. links Cuba with drug ring," *The Miami Herald*, January 27, 1982, p. 6.

18. Freemantle, *The Fix*, p. 256. Much of the following information on Nicaragua is based on United States Congress, Senate, Committee on Labor and Human Resources, *Role of Nicaragua in Drug Trafficking* (Washington, D.C.: Government Printing Office, 1985) and United States, House, Committee on Foreign Affairs, *Role of Nicaragua in Drug Trafficking* (Washington, D.C.: Government Printing Office, 1986).

19. Leslie Cockburn, *Out of Control.*

20. Brian Barger, "The Contras and Cocaine," *Penthouse*, December 1987, p. 166.

21. Timothy Ashby, *The Bear in the Back Yard*, p. 165.

22. Brian Freemantle, *The Fix*, p. 261.

23. Brian Barger, "The Contras and Cocaine," *Penthouse*, p. 168.

24. President's Commission on Organized Crime, *America's Habit*, p. 175.

25. Inter-American Development Bank, *Economic and Social Progress in Latin America 1983* (Washington, D.C.: Inter-American Development Bank, 1983), p. 275.

26. Inter-American Development Bank, *Economic and Social Progress in Latin America 1986* (Washington, D.C.: Inter-American Development Bank, 1986), pp. 322–323.

27. Ibid., p. 323.

28. "Inside the Sandinista Utopia," *The Latin American Times*, April 26, 1986, p. 12.

29. "Nicaragua: Betrayal of a worthy revolution," *The Latin American Times*, September 18, 1985, p. 24.

30. "Inside the Sandinista Utopia," *The Latin American Times*, p. 18.

# 9

# Avoiding the Eruption: Searching for Solutions

## INTRODUCTION

The Latin American drug trade is one of the major threats confronting the nations in the Western Hemisphere in the late twentieth century. In its wake has been rising addiction, societal disruption, and an increase in criminal and political violence. In certain cases, the drug trade has even challenged the existence of the state and its ability to govern.

This concluding chapter seeks to briefly review the major points of the preceding chapters and examine possible solutions. Considering the broad scope of the problem, the drug trade remains a volcano, threatening to erupt. This is a pessimistic conclusion, but unfortunately, true. At the same time, it is likely that the volcano will only continue to rumble and the societies of the Western Hemisphere will not be engulfed in a lava-flood of drug consumption that will lobotomize its youth. P. T. Barnum once said: "There's a sucker born every minute and two to grab him." With cocaine, marijuana, and heroin this is certainly true. The same could be said of legal drugs such as alcohol and tobacco. Unfortunately, there always will be "suckers" that will experiment with these substances and become addicted. The Latin American drug trade is here to stay, like it or not, as there will always be someone on the demand side willing to purchase and someone on the supply side, motivated either by greed or ideology, willing to sell. So the volcano will continue to rumble. There are, however, ways to prevent an eruption and mute those rumblings. First, it is useful to put the modern Latin American drug trade into a historical perspective.

## OTHER PLACES, OTHER TIMES: HISTORY REPEATING ITSELF

The Latin American drug trade is not an isolated event either historically or geographically. Nor are its offshoots, like narcoterrorism as reflected by the emergence of the Islamic revolutionary groups that grow and sell opium in Lebanon to finance their activities. Afghan rebels appear to be doing the same thing in their struggle against the Soviet-backed government in Kabul. In the distant past, history has recorded the role of illicit drugs in the decline of the Ching dynasty in China in the nineteenth century.

China under the Ching dynasty (1644–1911) had many of the same problems with opium that Latin and North American nations are having with cocaine, heroin, and marijuana. Though opium had been introduced into China as early as the 1600s by the Portuguese, it was not until 1729 that the Imperial government banned the use of the drug. Importation and domestic cultivation were also banned in 1796. Despite these measures and others, the smuggling of opium into the country was a highly lucrative enterprise for the British and North American shippers and their colleagues in the Chinese community. The spread of opium use throughout China became a part of the decline of the Ching dynasty. These negative factors are well worth reviewing for the nations of the Western Hemisphere. As Hsin-pao noted on the negative impact of opium on China:

The influx of opium into China on such a scale had far-reaching repercussions. It mobilized a large section of the population into active participation in law-defying pursuits: the grave social implications of this needs no further comment. Economically, the most conspicuous effect on the opium trade was the drain of silver specie, then China's main currency. As a result, commerce and finance in China were seriously handicapped. Furthermore, it not only contributed to the corruption of local governments and police forces, but also sapped the energy of the army and made useful active life impossible for a great many merchants, sailors, laborers, and others in all occupations. More and more people were being drawn away from normal, socially productive careers. In the end the Peking authorities could not help becoming alarmed.[1]

An additional element was that a number of anti-Ching secret societies were involved in the opium trade as a means of financing their revolutionary activities. The drug-insurgency existed in a different form and time.

It was only after the Chinese Communist Party under Mao Tse-tung came to power in 1949 that the drug problem was brought under control as a major societal problem. The Chinese Revolution was certainly a radical event and most nations in Latin America will not pursue that line of political development to solve the drug trade. China's tribulations with opium indicate that the current crisis is not an isolated historical development nor are many of its side effects substantially different. For countries like Colombia and Bolivia, the danger represented by the *narcotraficantes* represents the same destructive force that the opium trade and two opium wars had on China.

The China and Latin America drug experiences are not isolated. Britain and the United States had an earlier problem with opium and heroin addiction. United States efforts to curtail drug use began as early as 1875 when the city of San Francisco prohibited the operation of opium dens. Despite the passage of such laws as the Harrison Act in 1914, the consumption of the illicit drug was never completely eradicated. In all these cases, societies have sought to find solutions, which have encompassed both supply and demand approaches.

China's approach in the 1700s and 1800s was prohibition and interdiction. Neither was very successful. Eradication of drug use under the Communists was done with repressive techniques. Other Asian countries where drug use has been reduced include Malaysia, Singapore, and Taiwan. The former two have the death penalty for traffickers, which has been used to curtail activities. The Singapore model has been held up by some as the path out of the drug problem. While the death penalty deters traffickers (the supply side), stiff measures are imposed on the user (the demand side). Drug users in Singapore are treated as infectious agents and initially quarantined for six months. Detoxification is always "Cold Turkey" with no medicinal aid and the state has the legal right to extend the incarceration to thirty-six months.[2] Although this was successful in Singapore in halting what was becoming the spread of heroin use in the late 1970s, usage of drugs continues. Freemantle noted: "The crackdown has achieved impressive results, but Singapore is still not the drug-free haven that it would like to appear."[3] This author notes evidence of widespread cannabis abuse and psychotropics.

The Singaporean model of halting a heroin epidemic was relatively successful for Singapore. Does this model offer something for the United Staes and Latin American nations? The answer is negative. Singapore is a small city-state and the situation for local officials was easier. One of the major problems in the Americas is border control. In many cases, such as in Brazil, Colombia, and Bolivia, state control of the border is weak. Another important difference is much more fundamental and can be divided into three areas. One, Singaporean society is much more regimented and consensus-oriented than most of the nations in the Americas. Two, how could nations such as Bolivia and Jamaica, arrest and quarantine drug users, when drug use is so widely pervasive and cultural? Three, the Singaporean procedure of arresting addicts, taking a urine sample, and placing them in a rehabilitation center if they fail the test, raises serious questions about the constitutional rights of citizens in a Western democracy. In the United States, the activities of the drug treatment organization, Straight, Inc., with its philosophy of Toughlove, have raised similar questions concerning constitutional rights. Furthermore, many Latin nations have been newly re-democratized and such an approach as the Singaporean model would touch upon raw nerves.

If the approaches of prohibition, interdiction, and targeting the user are not applicable to the Americas, should drugs like cocaine and marijuana, be legalized? In a sense, coca consumption in the Andes and marijuana usage in Jamaica (not to mention in the United States) have been accepted by segments of society. There have been rumors from time to time that certain groups in Latin states have contemplated legalizing the external sale of cocaine beyond what is used by the legal drug industry. While Singapore represents a conservative supply and demand approach to dealing with drugs, Amsterdam represents the opposite.

The Netherlands has a long tradition of toleration and a willingness to conduct liberal societal experiments. Nowhere has this been more evident than in the case of drugs. For those in favor of some form of legalization as a means of control, the Dutch experiment is often cited. Arnold S. Trebach, a professor in the School of Justice, American University, and author of *The Heroin Solution*, favors this approach: "Thus the Dutch seem to have created a good model for the world."[4] Trebach admired the Dutch policy of not launching a "scorched-earth" policy against drugs, as he claims the United States did in 1986, but "consciously adopted a series of peaceful compromises and have rejected the idea of a war on drugs."[5]

Dutch authorities grew concerned about rising drug use in the 1970s. In 1976, a law was passed making it a misdemeanor, rather than a felony, to carry up to one and one-half ounces of marijuana for personal use. This was followed by a 1978 bill that permitted sales of cannabis at youth centers. The reasoning behind these bills was the Dutch philosophy that the criminalization of marijuana possession forced users into the criminal sphere in common with hard drugs, which were often sold in the same place and frequently by the same dealers.[6] The Dutch wanted to break the connection between soft and hard drugs. Lawyer Roelof Manschot, of the Dutch Ministry of Justice at the Hague stated: "Our policy towards marijuana is not one of legalization. It is one of recognizing the difference between hard and soft drugs and trying to prevent further escalation in the country. By making cannabis available in the controlled way we do, we feel it may be possible to keep them from turning to hard drugs."[7]

While the Dutch have largely "solved" their marijuana problem, in that it has been decriminalized, Amsterdam is well known as one of the drug capitals of Europe. Heroin addicts from the rest of Europe have been attracted to the city, which also has been lenient vis-à-vis hard drugs as well. According to Rosemary Brady in February, 1984: "Result: This city of tulips and canals has become one of Europe's street crime capitals as well as a haven for addicts."[8] Along these lines, the city of then 750,000 had 2,500 robberies, 50,000 pickpocketings and other petty thefts, 147 rapes, and 29 assault, of which the city's estimated 14,000 hard users were blamed for 90 percent.[9] This situation has hurt the country's tourist industry and has irritated a growing segment of Dutch society. While liberals, such as Trebach, advocate a Dutchlike approach, Detective Chief Superintendent Evert Jagerman at Warmoesstraat police headquarters, near Amsterdam's famous old red light district stated: "We have been too tolerant. We don't arrest users of heroin because there isn't enough capacity in the jails. People who steal get sent back on the street again. We arrest the same people over and over."[10]

Neither Singapore nor the Netherlands has fully resolved the problem of drug use in their respective societies, much like the beleagued Ching dynasty's failure at stopping the movement of opium into China in the eighteenth and nineteenth centuries. What was achieved in the two modern cases was better control over the inflow of drugs and making, intentionally and unintentionally, a delineation between soft and hard drugs.

What lessons can be drawn from the past for the Americas? First and foremost, historically antidrug campaigns have never been entirely successful in eradicating usage or production. Second, as Freemantle noted: "the truth of the history: that some people will always take drugs; that some actually *need* drugs."[11] Third, there is a need for governments to recognize that sad reality. A scorched-earth policy against all users of illegal drugs is beyond any government's capabilities. Even societies with high levels of societal control, such as the Soviet Union, have drug problems. If the Singaporean model were imposed, how would the United States quarantine an estimated 12 million heroin and cocaine users?[12]

Under certain circumstances, prescribed marijuana should be available for usage. These circumstances would include the terminally ill and patients with certain illnesses, such as glaucoma, where marijuana usage has been proven medicinal. This does not mean that marijuana should be legalized for wholesale, public distribution. This author disagrees with the contention that distinguishing marijuana from cocaine and heroin is a positive step. Government control of supply and demand through a state monopoly is not an answer. In France, the government has a monopoly on the sale of cigarettes and antismoking campaigns have collided head-on against the possibility of reduced government revenues. If the state is going to sell, then it is condoning the damaging effects of narcotics use. Is that the right message to send? Should the state promote a lifestyle based on drug use? I fully concur with the conclusion of a study by the Organization of American States:

Narcotics drugs identified by the International Narcotic Control Boards are prohibited substances because of their threat to people and their societies. There is no debate about their effects, and to legalize them would give them a status which is contrary to the terms and provisions at the UN Single Convention on Narcotics Drugs; such action would at best confuse the public, especially the young. And, there can be no assurance that legalization and its processes would achieve the objectives sought.[13]

## WHAT SHOULD BE DONE?

Hard and soft drugs pose serious challenges to American societies. What, then should be done? They should not be decriminalized or legalized. Both supply and demand approaches are required, ranging from crop eradication (on the supply side) to greater public awareness. The antidrug campaign conducted by first lady Nancy Reagan was a step in the right direction, but more is needed and in different forms. There is a need for greater coordination of United States policy because several branches of government are involved, including Customs, the military, the State Department, and the Drug Enforcement Agency. In a sense, the number of agencies involved in the struggle have unintentionally made the development and implementation of a coherent policy difficult. What is necessary is the creation of a drug czar, whose position should be a cabinet post reporting to the president. The czar should be empowered to bring under one chain of command and direction United States drug policy. The office could be brought into legislation with a sunset amendment (which could be renewed if necessary) and would liason among the governmental agencies to streamline and formulate policy actions.

The drug czar would begin a campaign of greater public awareness. The importance of greater public awareness in the Americas was emphasized by the Organization of American States: "What is required is a mass mobilization of consciousness about the effects of drug use and an involvement of every sector of the community, from family to school, from workplace to social club in a sustained program to discourage experimentation with, tolerance, and consumption of narcotics."[14] Special attention should be given to the United States, the major market.

Certain of the suggestions made by the Organization of American States conference on the traffic in narcotics are worthwhile considering. It should be emphasized that these are soft options, underlining community participation. To paraphrase these in a broad fashion, an inter-

American clearinghouse should be established through which a steady flow of information, experiences, ideas and programs could be exchanged. There should be the promotion of community-level organizations in every major district of every city, town and village of the Americas which could mobilize school, church, neighborhood, medical center, and social clubs to join the fight against drug usage.

There is a pressing need for an improvement of statistical and epidemiological information on drug use, especially on the patterns of consumption. This need is due to the scarcity of data about how drugs are administered, in what dosages, and frequency of use. Both for prevention and treatment, an enhancement of knowledge would greatly facilitate effective action.

There has already been some movement along these lines, in the form of joint efforts between Latin and Caribbean governments against *narcotraficantes* as a core policy objective. Enforcement has benefitted from a greater sharing of intelligence, joint maneuvers in drug-producing regions, and an upgrading of extradition treaties between nations. Already, Colombia, Brazil, and Peru have conducted coordinated antidrug campaigns in their mutually shared border regions, and meetings have been held between the countries' respective drug enforcement police. The United States has actively conducted missions with Bolivia, Mexico, the Bahamas, and Jamaica.

The OAS also supports a strengthening of enforcement measures. Some of the better conceived ideas include: more frequent regional and interregional training seminars and workshops for drug law enforcement personnel; provision of rapid, secure and direct means of communication; and establishment of bilateral agreements between states with common problems arising from the illicit traffic. United States support in joint efforts is also important—especially so—considering the country's greater enforcement resources. United States support for antinarcotics forces in the Americas along these lines remains highly important. Though there is a delicate line to be tread between actual United States troop involvement in armed clashes with Latin and Caribbean *narcotraficantes* and the providing of logistical support to local enforcement on Bolivia, United States military involvement can play a positive role. It should be added also that this option is to be used only upon the invitation of another country. Along these lines, Washington should provide Latin and Caribbean governments with the technical means of improving their strategic reach. Renssaler W. Lee III noted: "Latin governments still will need better weapons, transport, communications systems, and support services."[15]

The development of greater regional cooperation against the drug trade hinges largely upon relations between the United States and its Latin American neighbors. There has traditionally been a love-hate relationship between the northern and southern hemispheres, which has, more than once, led to mutual suspicion and hostility. The Latin American drug trade calls for both North and South Americans to rise above the various periods of estrangement, and work together in a mature relationship. The equation is simple: the drug trade negatively effects *all* nations in the Americas—should not the problem be brought under control by *all* (or most) of those same nations?

Innovative new measures that are mutually reinforcing are needed. Moreover, other issues and problems that confront Latin American and Caribbean economic development and legal trade must be linked. Lee noted:

The United States has to integrate narcotics control with its other hemispheric priorities. Tradeoffs may be unavoidable, at least in the short term. The experience of Colombia and Bolivia suggest that antidrug measures may harm a country financially by driving dollars from the banking system, thus reducing the value of the local currency and worsening debt problems.[16]

While the concept of a Common Market of the Americas remains distant, measures must be taken to strengthen legal economies by pushing back the forces of protectionism and advancing, in a gradualistic fashion, greater free trade. Protectionism, in itself, is a dangerous force, but in the drug trade, it is negative reinforcement in the movement from legal products to illicit products. The subsidization of, and ongoing, cuts in the United States sugar quota system in the 1980s for example, has been a key force in pushing Belizean and Jamaican cultivators out of sugar and into marijuana cultivation. In Bolivia, the near bankruptcy of the economy that related to the downturn in tin prices (hurt in part by subsidization around the world and the development of chemical substitutes) led local *campesinos* to turn to coca production. Often overlooked as a core element of the Latin American drug trade, economic development (or the lack of) is a significant factor in making the illegal narcotics trade tempting.

## A DEBT-DRUGS SOLUTION?

One possible option not yet attempted is to link debt and drugs together in an antinarcotic package. This is not to argue that the Latin debt crisis is the cause of the drug trade in the Americas. It is, however, part of the problem as austerity programs often deplete law enforcement agency budgets, reduce already low salaries, and drive down the nation's standard of living. These conditions, in turn, cause a lack of resources to launch and sustain effective antinarcotics campaigns and to open the door to official corruption. Outside of the impact on regional enforcement agencies, difficult economic conditions enhance the attractiveness of the drug trade. In many countries where legal employment is low, the cultivation, refining and export of cocaine, marijuana, heroin, and synthetic drugs provides a livelihood. Legitimate economic enterprises, seeded with narcomoney, also provide employment and income. For most individuals involved in the drug industry, economic survival is the essential reason for involvement. At higher levels, greed is clearly the motive.

There have been a number of instances where Latin *narcotraficantes* have offered to repay the country's external debt in return for amnesty. As of mid–1988 there have been no takers, at least publicly among the governments in Latin America and the Caribbean. The offer, however, is tempting. For a pardon, one of the most significant obstacles to national development could be removed. Governments have balked for fear of international reaction and possible long-term impact by officially acknowledging the power of the *narcotraficantes*. Free to move in society, would they seek to mobilize their wealth and influence into the formal political system in presidential races? What would happen to a nation with a *narcotraficante* elected as chief executive? Nations with *narcotraficantes* in positions of authority, as in Panama with General Noriega, have found this situation difficult.

An option to negate the sirenlike allure of narcomoney being used to repay external obligations is to adopt a program that links debt reduction and narcotics enforcement. Countries that pursue antidrugs campaigns can have the United States government purchase portions of their debt on the secondary market and give it to them as a form of antinarcotics assistance. This would mean that if the United States wanted to assist Mexico with its antidrug program, $10 million of Mexican debt could be bought on the secondary market where the value of that country's debt has an actual worth of under 50 cents for each dollar at face value. Officially $20 million of Mexican debt paper would be given to the Mexican government, which could then put that capital to use inside the country. The result achieved: Mexico's official debt would be reduced by $20 million, and the United States would help a friendly government combat its drug problem. Moreover, the United States would help strengthen its financial system by a healthier Mexico capable of repaying its debt to the United States banks.

The packaging of a debt reduction-antidrugs program would bring other important benefits. For many countries, an additional item on the new debt-reduction menu will help them make advances in the overall economy and, hopefully, improve the standard of living. Improved living conditions, fiscally stronger states, and improved enforcement agencies with greater reach would provide a stronger bulwark against the spread of the drug-insurgency nexus and narcoterrorism. Especially important under this approach is investment in rural modernization.[17] Rural modernization in this sense was defined by Kempe Ronald Hope: "The cardinal aim of rural development is viewed not simply as agricultural and economic growth in the narrow sense, but as balanced social and economic development, including the generation of new employment; the equitable distribution of income; widespread improvement in health, nutrition, and housing; greatly broadened opportunities for all individuals to realize their full potential through education; and a strong voice for all rural people in shaping the decisions and actions that affect their lives."[18] As it has been in the hard-to-reach country areas that the drug-insurgency nexus has developed, the preconditions for that development must be eradicated. This can be done through either direct financial assistance or, as suggested here, by debt-equity swaps linked to antinarcotics programs.

The Latin American drug trade has an impact on all nations in the Western Hemisphere and reaches into each society, influencing, in some fashion, the political and economic climates. It remains an angry volcano, threatening to blow its roof off, inundating the nations below it with a lava flood of drugs. In the 1970s and early 1980s, many danced on the volcano, somewhat oblivious to the danger or, in some cases, arguing that it was someone else's worry, not theirs. The rumbles grew louder and louder and the dancing on the volcano ceased. In the late 1980s and 1990s, the question lingers—will the correct measures be taken to release some of the pressure and avoid what will be a nasty eruption? Much hinges on the political will of the leadership elite throughout the region.

## NOTES

1. Hsin-pao Chang, *Commissioner Lin and the Opium War* (New York: W.W. Norton and Company, Inc., 1964), p. 32. Also see Li Chien-nung, *The Political History of China 1840–1928* (Stanford: Stanford University Press, 1956), pp. 26–33.

2. Brian Freemantle, *The Fix: Inside the World Drug Trade* (New York: Tom Doherty Associates, Inc., 1986), p. 171.

3. Ibid.

4. Arnold S. Trebach, *The Great Drug War: And Radical Proposals That Could Make America Safe Again* (New York: MacMillan Publishing Company, 1978), p. 106.

5. Ibid., pp. 103–104.

6. Ibid., p. 104.

7. Quoted in Brian Freemantle, *The Fix*, pp. 192–193.

8. Rosemary Brady, "In Dutch," *Forbes*, February 27, 1984, p. 46.

9. Ibid.

10. Ibid.

11. Brian Freemantle, *The Fix*, p. 315.

12. *Washington Post*, June 28, 1987, p. A26.

13. Organization of American States, "Socio-Economic Studies for the Inter-American Specialized Conference on Drug Traffic," Inter-American Specialized Conference on Traffic in Narcotics Drugs. (Washington, D.C.: Organization of American States, April 22, 1986), p. 74.

14. Ibid., p. 75.

15. Renssaler W. Lee III, "The Latin American Drug Connection," *Foreign Policy*, (Winter 1985–86), No. 61, p. 159.

16. Ibid., p. 158.

17. Ibid., p. 159.

18. Kempe Ronald Hope, *Economic Development in the Caribbean* (New York: Praeger Publishers, 1986), pp. 62–63.

# Bibliography

## BOOKS

Ashby, Timothy. *The Bear in the Back Yard: Moscow's Caribbean Policy*. Lexington, Mass.: Lexington Books, 1987.

Bailey, Norman A. and Richard Cohen. *The Mexican Time Bomb*, New York: Priority Press Publications, 1987.

Bascopé Aspiazu, René. *La Veta Blanca: Coca y Cocaina en Bolivia*. La Paz: Ediciónes Aqui, 1982.

Berry, Albert, Ronald H. Hellman and Maurcicio Soluan. (editors). *Politics of Compromise: Coalition Government in Colombia*. New Brunswick, N.J.: Transaction Press, 1980.

Brown, Kendall W. *Bourbons and Brandy: Imperial Reform in Eighteenth-Century Arequipa*. Albuquerque: University of New Mexico Press, 1986.

Camp, Roderic A. (editor). *Mexico's Political Stability: The Next Five Years*. Boulder, Colo.: Westview Press, 1986.

Campbell, Horace. *Rasta and Resistance: From Marcus Garvey to Walter Rodney*. Trenton, N.J.: New Africa Press, 1987.

Canelas, Amando and Juan Carlos Canelas Zannier. *Bolivia: Coca, cocaína*. Cochabamba, Bolivia: Los Amigos del Libro, 1983.

Carias Sisco, German. *La Mafia de la Cocaína*. Caracas: Ediciónes de Información y Relaciones Públicas del Ministerio de Justícia y Guardia Nacional, 1986).

Castillo, Fabio. *Los Jinetes de la Cocaína* (Bogotá: Editorial Documentos Periodicistas, 1977).

Cespedes, Guillermo. *Latin America: The Early Years*. New York: Alfred A. Knopf, 1974.

Chang, Hsin-pao, *Commissioner Lin and the Opium War*. New York: W.W. Norton and Company, 1964.

Cockburn, Leslie. *Out of Control: The Story of the Reagan Administration's Secret*

*War in Nicaragua, the Illegal Arms Pipeline, and the Contra Drug Connection* New York: Atlantic Monthly Press, 1987.

Crabtree, John, Gavan Duffy and Jenny Pearce. *The Great Tin Crash: Bolivia and the World Tin Market.* London: Latin America Bureau, 1987.

Crosby, Alfred W., Jr. *The Colombia Exchange: Biological and Cultural Consequences of 1492.* Westport, Conn.: Greenwood Press, 1972.

Diaz, Bernal. *The Conquest of New Spain.* New York: Penguin Books, 1963.

Dix, Robert H. *The Politics of Colombia.* New York: Praeger Publishers, 1987.

Dobyns, Henry E. and Paul L. Doughty, *Peru: A Cultural History.* New York: Oxford University Press, 1976.

Dolan, Edward F. *International Drug Traffic.* New York: F. Watts, 1985.

Dreher, Melanie Creagen. *Working Men and Ganja: Marijuana Use in Rural Jamaica* Philadelphia: Institute for the Study of Human Issues, 1982.

Dunkerly, James. *Rebellion in the Veins: Political Struggle in Bolivia, 1952–1982.* London: Verso Editions, 1984.

Eddy, Paul. *The Cocaine Wars.* New York: W.W. Norton, 1988.

Freemantle, Brian, *The Fix: Inside the World Drug Trade.* New York: Tom Doherty Associates, 1986.

Gutiérrez Anzola, Jorge. *Violencia y Justícia.* Bogotá, Colombia: Ediciones Tercer Mundo, 1962.

Hemming, John. *The Conquest of the Incas.* New York: Harcourt Brace Jovanovich, 1970.

Henman, Anthony, Roger Lewis and Tim Malyon. (editors). *Big Deal: The Politics of the Illicit Drug Business.* London: Pluto Press, 1985.

Horowitz, Michael M. (editor), *Peoples and Cultures of the Caribbean: An Anthropological Reader.* Garden City, N.Y.: Natural History Press, 1971.

Kempe, Ronald Hope. *Economic Development in the Caribbean.* New York: Praeger Publishers, 1986.

Lacey, Terry. *Violence and Politics in Jamaica, 1960–70: Internal Security in a Developing Country.* Totowa, N.J.: Frank Cass & Co., 1977.

Li Chein-nung. *The Political History of China, 1840–1928.* Stanford, Cal.: Stanford University Press, 1956.

Lowenthal, Abraham. *Partners in Conflict: The United States and Latin America.* Baltimore: Johns Hopkins University Press, 1987.

Lupsha, Peter A. and Kip Schlegal. *The Political Economy of Drug Trafficking: The Herrera Organization (Mexico and the United States).* Albuquerque: Latin American Institute, University of New Mexico, 1980.

Malcolm, Andrew. *Pursuit of Intoxication.* Toronto, Ontario: Addiction Research Foundation, 1971.

Malloy, James A. and Richard S. Thorn. (editors). *Beyond the Revolution: Bolivia Since 1952.* Pittsburgh: University of Pittsburgh Press, 1971.

McNicoll, Andre. *Drug Trafficking: a North-South Perspective* Ottawa, Ontario: North-South Institute, 1983.

Mills, James. *The Underground Empire: Where Crime and Governments Embrace.* Garden City, New York: Doubleday & Co., 1986.

Newell, Roberto G. and Luis Rubio F. *Mexico's Dilemma: The Political Origins of Economic Crisis.* Boulder, Colo.: Westview Press, 1984.

Pacini, Deborah and Christine Franquemont. (editors). *Coca and Cocaine: Effects on People and Policy in Latin America*. Petersborough, New Hampshire: Transcript Printing Company, 1986.

Park, Yoon S. and Jack Zwick. *International Banking Theory and Practice*. Reading, Mass.: Addison-Wesley Publishing Company, 1985.

Ponce Caballero, A. Gaston. *Coca, Cocaína, Tráfico* La Paz, Bolivia: Empresa El Diario, 1983.

Riding, Alan. *Distant Neighbors: A Portrait of the Mexicans*. New York: Alfred A. Knopf, 1985.

Segal, Bernard. *Cocaine*. New York: Gardner Press, 1988.

Trebach, Arnold S. *The Great Drug War: And Radical Proposals That Could Make America Safe Again*. New York: MacMillan Publishing Company, 1987.

Walters, Anita W. *Race, Class and Political Symbols: Rastafari and Reggae*. New Brunswick, N.J.: Transaction Books, 1985.

Whitaker, Morris D. *The Status of Bolivian Agriculture*. New York: Praeger Publishers, 1975.

Young, Alma H. and Dion E. Philips. (editors). *Militarization in the Non-Hispanic Caribbean*. Boulder, Colo.: Lyne Rienner Publishers, 1986.

## ARTICLES

Aguilar Zinser, Adolfo. "Mexico: The Presidential Problem." *Foreign Policy* (Winter 1987–88).

Barger, Brian, "The Contras and Cocaine." *Penthouse* (December 1987).

Bogdanowicz-Bindert, Christine A. "World Debt: The United States Reconsiders." *Foreign Affairs* 64: 2 (Winter 1985–86), pp. 259–273.

Brady, Rosemary. "In Dutch." *Forbes*, February 27, 1984, p. 46.

Castaneda, Jorge G. "Mexico at the Brink." *Foreign Affairs* 64: 2 (Winter 1985–86), pp. 287–303.

Christian, Shirley, "Bolivia Is Hoping U.S. Drug Forces Will Extend Stay." *The New York Times*, August 22, 1986, p. A1 and B4.

de Onis, Juan. "Mexican Farmers Discover Big Money in Grass." *The New York Times*, September 18, 1969, p. 1.

———. "Drug Watch on Mexico Adding to Latin Disillusion With Nixon." *The New York Times*, October 8, 1969, p. 17.

Diehl, Jackson. "Surge in Cocaine Traffic Sparks Venezuelan Antidrug Campaign." *Washington Post*, November 22, 1984, p. 8.

Durr, Barbara. "Drugs War Create Dilemma for Bolivia." *The Financial Times*, August 20, 1986, p. 4.

Eckstein, S. "El capitalismo mundial y la revolución agraria en Bolivia." *Revista Mexicana de Sociologia*, vol. XLI (1979), pp. 457–478.

Galloway, Johnathan F. and Maria Velez de Berliner. "The Worldwide Illegal Cocaine Industry." (Paper presented at the 28th Annual Convention of the International Studies Association, Washington D.C., April 15–18, 1987).

Gardner, David. "Mexico protests to US over drug trafficking claims." *The Financial Times*, May 15, 1987, p. 5.

Gillespie, Doreen. "Peru Agriculture Minister Resigns." *Financial Times*, January 8, 1986, p. 4.

Graham, Bradley. "Colombian Supreme Court Overturns Extradition Pact With U.S." *The Washington Post*, June 27, 1987, p. A16.

———. *"Cease-Fire Toters in Colombia."* *The Washington Post*, July 6, 1987, p. A13.

Hanna, Joel M. and C.A. Hornick. "Use of Coca Leaf in Southern Peru: Adaptation or Addiction." *Bulletin of Narcotics* 29:1, (1977), pp. 63–74.

Herrin, Angela. "Latins Divert Land; Plant Coca, Not Corn," *Journal of Commerce*, October 18, 1985, p. 4.

Hiaasen, Carl. "Bahamas Charged with Drug Payoffs." *Miami Herald*, October 30, 1983, p. 6.

James, Canute. "Drug Smugglers Turn to Caribbean Island-hopping." *The Financial Times*, November 13, 1987, p. 5.

Kelly, Nicki. "Bahamas PM survives after pledge of respectability." *The Financial Times*, October 30, 1984, p. 4.

*Latin American Regional Reports Andean*, June 24, 1983, pp. 7–8.

Lee, Rensseler W., III. "The Latin American Drug Connection." *Foreign Policy* (Winter 1985–86), No. 61, pp. 142–159.

Leiber, James. "Coping with Cocaine." *The Atlantic Monthtly* (January 1986).

Mann, Joe. "Venezuela Crackdown on Border Crime." *The Financial Times*, January 12, 1988, p. 4.

Maranto, Gina. "Coke: the Random Killer." *Discover* (March 1986).

Martin, Richard T., "The Role of Coca in the History, Religion, and Medicine of South American Indians." *Economic Botany* vol. 24: (1970), pp. 422–438.

Nares, Peter. "Marxist Guerrillas Strike Out at Colombia's Jugular." *The Wall Street Journal*, January 23, 1987, p. 23.

———. "Colombian Guerrillas Drug Connections Crystallize in Shootout." *The Wall Street Journal*. November 15, 1987, p. 31.

Neyist, Rod. "Guyana 1988: Drugs and Garbage." *Friends of Jamaica Caribbean Newsletter*, 8: 1, February-March 1988, p. 1.

Riding, Alan. "Peru's Forces Press Ahead in Drug War." *The New York Times*, August 17, 1986, p. A12.

Roett, Riordan. "Peru: The Message from Garcia." *Foreign Affairs* 64: 2 (Winter 1985–86), p. 251.

Solo, Tova Maria. "U.S. Protectionism Fires Up Colombia Drug Farmers." *The Wall Street Journal*, November 14, 1986, p. 31.

Stockton, William. "Mexico's Drug effort Will also be Home Grown." *The New York Times*, August 17, 1986, p. 26.

———. "Mexico is Top US Source of Heroin." *The Washington Post*, February 22, 1986, p. A20.

Taylor, Frank Fonda. "Does Trinidad Have a Drug Problem?" *Caribbean Review* XV:4 (Winter 1987–88): 15.

Thornton, Mary. "A Murder at the Border of No-Man's Land." *The Washington Post*, February 22, 1986, p. A4.

Treaster, Joseph B. "Colombian troops are said to break courthouse seige." *The New York Times*, November 8, 1985, p. 1.

Webb, Craig. "Treasury Sets Rules to Trace Drug Money." *The Washington Post*, April 7, 1987, p. E4.

Weinraud, Bernard. "Reagan Urged to Meet Latin Chiefs on Drugs." *The New York Times*, March 18, 1987, p. A10.

"What is our Drug Problem? Forum," *Harpers*, December, 1985, pp. 39–51.

Williams, Edward J. "The Implications of the Border for Mexico Policy and Mexican-United States Relations." In Roderic A. Camp (editor). *Mexico's Political Stability: The Next Five Years*. Boulder, Colo.: Westview Press, 1986.

Wheeler, Linda and Keith Harriston. "Jamaican Gangs Wage War Over Drugs, Area Police Say." *The Washington Post*, November 19, 1987, p. A18.

Yanez Orozco, Jesus. "The Fight Against the Drug Trade." *Voices of Mexico* (September-November, 1986), p. 52.


## PRIMARY SOURCES

Bahamas. Report of the Commission of Inquiry appointed to Dangerous Drugs Destined for the United States of America, *Report of the Commission of Inquiry, Appointed to Inquire into the Illegal Use of the Bahamas for the Transshipment of Dangerous Drugs Destined for the United States of America, November-December 1983*. Nassau, Bahamas: Government of the Bahamas, 1984.

Economist Intelligence Unit. *Quarterly Economic Review of Peru, Bolivia*, No. 1, 1983.

———. *Quarterly Economic Review of Peru, Bolivia*, No. 2, 1983.

Excelsior. "Mexico: An Exclusive Interview with Miguel de al Madrid," *Excelsior*, Mexico City, July 1984.

———. *Economic and Social Progress in Latin America 1987 Report*. Washington, D.C.: Inter-American Development Bank, 1987.

Inter-American Development Bank. *Economic and Social Progress in Latin America 1983 Report*. Washington, D.C.: Inter-American Development Bank, 1983.

———. *Economic and Social Progress in Latin America 1986 Report*, Washington, D.C.: Inter-American Development Bank, 1986.

International Monetary Fund. *International Financial Statistics Yearbook 1986*. Washington D.C.: International Monetary Fund, 1986.

National Task Force on Drug Abuse in the Bahamas. *Report of the National Task Force on Drug Abuse in the Bahamas*. Nassau: Bahamas Printing Office, 1984.

Organization for Economic Cooperation and Development. *Extra Debt Statistics: The Debt and Other External Liabilities of Developing, CMEA and Certain Other Countries and Territories*. Paris: Organization for Economic Cooperation and Development, 1987.

Perticioli, Gustavo. "Address to the Third Annual Meeting of National Banks, Guadalajara, Jallisco, Mexico, July 9, 1987." *Banamex: Review of the Economic Situation of Mexico* (Mexico City), vol. LXII, no. 740 (July 1987), pp. 171–174.

President's Commission on Organized Crime. *America's Habit: Drug Abuse, Drug Trafficking and Organized Crime*. Washington, D.C.: U.S. Government Printing Office, March 1986.

Secretary of Health and Human Services. *Report to Congress: Drug Abuse and Drug Abuse Research*. Washington, D.C.: U.S. Government Printing Office, 1984.

United States Congress, House. *Hearings to Create a Select Committee on Narcotics Abuse and Control Before House Committee on Rules and Administration*. Washington, D.C.: 96th Congress, 2nd session, 1980.

United States Congress, House, Committee on Foreign Affairs. *Role of Nicaragua in Drug Trafficking*. Washington, D.C.: Government Printing Office, 1986.

United States Congress, House, Committee on Foreign Affairs Task Force on International Narcotics Control. *Narcotics Production and Transshipment in Belize and Central America*. Washington, D.C.: Government Printing Office, 1985.

United States Congress, Senate, Committee on Labor and Human Resources, Subcommittee on Children, Drugs, and Alcoholism. *Role of Nicaragua in Drug Trafficking*. Washington, D.C.: Government Printing Office, 1985.

United States Senate, Permanent Subcommittee on Investigations of the Committee on Governmental Affairs. *Crime and Secrecy: The Use of Offshore Banks and Companies*. Washington, D.C.: Government Printing Office, 1985.

World Bank. *World Bank Development Report 1987*. New York: Oxford University Press, 1987.

World Bank. *Panama: Structural Change and Growth Prospects*. Washington, D.C.: The World Bank, 1985.

# Index

## ABOUT THE AUTHOR

SCOTT B. MACDONALD is the chief international economist at Maryland National Corporation International Bank. Prior to that, he was the senior international economist at American Security Bank in Washington, D.C. (1986–87) and the unit manager for international and specialized industries in the loan administration at Connecticut National Bank in Hartford, Connecticut (1985–86). He has also worked as the press secretary and deputy campaign manager for a congressional campaign in Connecticut and as a teaching assistant at the University of Connecticut. He received his doctorate in political science from the University of Connecticut in 1985, his master's degree in area studies from the University of London's School of Oriental and African Studies, and his bachelor's degree from Trinity College in Connecticut.

Dr. MacDonald has written over 100 articles, appearing in such publications as *The Times of the Americas, Journal of Interamerican Studies and World Affairs,* and *Caribbean Review.* He is also the author of *Trinidad and Tobago: Democracy and Development in the Caribbean* (1986) and coauthor of *The Caribbean After Grenada: Revolution, Conflict and Democracy* (forthcoming 1988). Currently, he is working on a fourth book, *The Caribbean Basin Sugar Crisis: A Descent into Hell.*